BRIEFCASE WISDOM

for a

BACKPACK CULTURE

JERRY GANO

WESTBOW
PRESS®
A DIVISION OF THOMAS NELSON
& ZONDERVAN

WestBow Press books may be ordered through booksellers or by contacting:

WestBow Press
A Division of Thomas Nelson & Zondervan
1663 Liberty Drive
Bloomington, IN 47403
www.westbowpress.com
1 (866) 928-1240

ISBN: 978-1-9736-7568-6 (sc)
ISBN: 978-1-9736-7569-3 (hc)
ISBN: 978-1-9736-7567-9 (e)

Library of Congress Control Number: 2019915004

Print information available on the last page.

WestBow Press rev. date: 10/03/2019

Introduction

For over five years, God has directed me to post on social media daily. Some 1,800 social media posts later, my goal has been and continues to be to edify and build the kingdom of God. I am merely a man, and I have written a few duds—and possibly a few gems. Most are a compelling message each day to those who would read the words that God gives to me. God has inspired me to share with others what He has placed in my heart.

I am sharing my story as life unfolds before me. I experience trials, heartache, sickness, pain, and life situations, and I am attacked by the enemy of my soul in similar ways that everyone is. This I know: if God goes before me, who can stand against me? I am nothing, in and of myself, but with God leading and directing my path, everything turns out okay. Yes, I have battles that are like what so many others face, but if the devil says something, I know that it's a lie for he cannot tell the truth. And if God says something, it is pure truth because He cannot lie. God's Word declares that truth sets us free. Indeed, I am free and glad to express it here on these pages.

January 1

Briefcase or Backpack

Psalm 119:9–16

We live in a backpack world. As the title of this book suggests, there is much wisdom that a "briefcase" generation can share with a "backpack" generation. When I was a young adult, businessmen carried briefcases. Today, I have a briefcase in which I carry my computer and important papers and a backpack for other activities. I recently received a backpack fishing tacklebox for my use when fishing. Today is a "backpack" culture. Many businesspeople wear backpacks as a carryover from school backpacks. It's amazing what is carried in these backpacks. Certainly, the computer and other electronic devices are there but also lunch, drinks, snacks, books, support materials for the job or school, and much more. As Christians, let's make sure that we include God's Word in our briefcases or backpacks. God's Word may be accessed on the computer, iPad, iPhone, and most other electronic devices. Let's be sure it is part of what we carry with us every day in life, whether for work or pleasure. Don't leave home without it! Briefcase or backpack: I still use both, and God's Word fits well into them.

January 2

Everyday Lessons from Life

Psalm 25:1–7

As I read the stories of Jesus's ministry while He walked on this earth, I am amazed at how He used the everyday things of life to teach spiritual lessons. I have found that, in part, God has led me to do the same with these thoughts that I write each day. When

Jesus and the disciples were walking by a wheat field, Jesus taught about a seed falling to the ground, dying, and creating new life. Jesus walked by a barren fig tree, and as He did so a second time, He spoke death to it for not being fruitful. So many parables and stories of life and spiritual truth! I enjoy sharing the experience of life as it occurs. No, it is not all good; I have bad experiences. But through it all, I have found God to be continually faithful, extending new mercy to me each day. Lord God Almighty, help me to continue to see spiritual lessons from what I experience in life, and help me to share them with the world of people who need to hear the good news of Jesus's salvation.

January 3

God Delights in Orchestrating My Life

Jeremiah 29:11

This morning, one of my young friends posted this thought: "I wish God would give me a road map or something."

I replied, "God delights in leading us one step at a time, one day at a time. Trust God! He is having fun."

As I have contemplated this dialogue between my young friend and me, I recognize that God has given humankind a desire to do wonderful things for others—in secret. Usually, there is a lot of hidden background work that goes into efforts like a surprise party or a surprise visit. When I participate in one of these functions, I enjoy seeing the expressions of the one being surprised.

I do believe that God is having fun in leading us, one step at a time, down a road we have never traveled. God takes great delight in planning our lives. He is preparing some great surprises for us. God wants to do us good, not harm, all the days of our lives.

Enjoy the walk! I'm pretty sure there are some good surprises ahead.

An Advocate

1 John 2:1

As I understand the Word of God, there will come a time when all people who have lived upon this earth will stand before almighty God, Creator of all things, and give an account for everything done in their lives while here on the earth. All truth will be present, and for those who never accepted Jesus Christ as Savior, every deed, lie, sin, and refusal to accept Jesus will be exposed. They will have no advocate, lawyer, friend, or family member to help them as they stand accused before the throne of God. God's supreme judgment is all that awaits them.

For the child of God whose life has been redeemed, that time of accountability includes having an advocate, Jesus Christ, our Savior, standing with us before almighty God. Jesus not only stands with us but also tells the heavenly Father about all the sin that was covered by His blood poured out at the cross. All the sinful past that could have condemned us for eternity is now covered by the blood of our Savior. We are no longer condemned but redeemed and stand before almighty God in the righteousness of Jesus, our Savior.

Which do you choose: eternity condemned forever or covered with Jesus Christ's righteousness in God's heaven? I choose righteousness. Will you?

January 5

This Is God's Day

Psalm 118:19–24

Today is Sunday. It's not just another Sunday. It is this Sunday, a day that the Lord has made. God tells us that His mercies are new every morning. Almighty God, thank you for those new mercies on this a brand-new Sunday—the Lord's day! It's the beginning of a brand-new week. I love beginnings! Last week is fading into the past. I can't change any part of it, but I can start this and every week out right by being in the Lord's house on the Lord's day. Thank you, God, for these new mercies. You knew that I would have need of them! This, the Lord's day, is the day that You have made, and I will rejoice and be glad in it!

January 6

God Changed My Life

1 Corinthians 6:9–11

A songwriter penned the words, "Who I am ain't who I was!" I am so thankful that God changes us for much better when He gets hold of us. God is simply in the business of *life changing.* His delight is not in punishment or revealing His wrath. God's delight is in bringing positive and beneficial change into the lives of all who serve Him. Yesterday, there were some tough and even terrible times, but consider that the Potter molds the clay and then places it into the fire for the perfect vessel that He desires. I may be on the Potter's wheel or perhaps even just a lump of clay—or I may be in the fire—but I am confident of this: God makes no mistakes. What each of us goes through is God creating a masterpiece—a unique and perfect masterpiece. I love what I am seeing God do in the lives of others and in my life as He has fun in the pottery shop!

January 7

The Outcome of Expectation

Philippians 1:19–21

Expectation is a powerful influence in our lives. Each of us has dwelled on expectations that have come true and yielded exactly what was desired, and just as dramatic are the expectations that have yielded disappointment. Expectation often employs hard work and persistence. I have watched my wife, LaDonna, do a lot of baking over the years. When she asks what kind of pie I want, and I reply apple, my expectation is kindled as I anticipate the result. It doesn't occur at the snap of fingers or just speaking it into being. I can't just throw flour, sugar, cinnamon, apples, and butter into a pie pan, put it into an oven, and get what I expect. Yes, it's all there but not to my expectation. The flour and other crust ingredients must be blended together and then rolled out into a crust of perfect thickness. The filling requires the apples to be peeled and sliced to just the right thickness and the sugar, cinnamon, butter, and other ingredients to be mixed together and placed into the pie shell. And then another crust is placed on top, with some vent holes to allow steam to escape. It must stay in the oven for the prescribed time and then be taken out and allowed to cool a bit before I slice it and put two large scoops of ice cream alongside it. Now it meets my expectation!

Sometimes we have great expectations from God. Yes, I believe in miracles, but sometimes I believe that God wants us in the "kitchen," working toward fulfilling our expectations. I am excited about the expectation that God has placed in my heart. I'm willing to work toward seeing that expectation fulfilled as I dream it in my heart.

January 8

The Sin of Trading Truth for Lies

Romans 1:1–32

The apostle Paul shares this fact in the first chapter of Romans: "They traded the Truth of God for lies." There are some things about the "Truth of God" that must be stated. First, God, in His position of Creator God, cannot lie. All truth is in Him. If God states it, then it is truth. If the devil says it, then it's a lie or at best a half truth. Why would I desire to accept a lie in place of the truth? It's my sin nature to desire what is a lie. But my God nature, birthed within me when I accepted Jesus as Lord of my life, demands the truth. Jesus said, "The Truth will set you free." If that is true—and it is—then the reverse is true as well. Lies will make you a prisoner!

Our world and culture are plagued with untruths. Lies are the immorality of our culture that we must accept as a movement that says God accepts humankind's changing of the Word of God to allow for sin. No! God's truth is this: God loves each individual. He loves each one so much that He sent His only begotten Son to die in our place—to die for our sins—so that we could experience repentance and forgiveness of sin and become new creations in Christ Jesus.

In Jesus, old things die, and behold—all things become new! That's the truth!

January 9

Are You Prepared?

Matthew 24:43–44

While the moisture is welcome, the icy conditions are making travel extremely difficult and causing lots of property damage and power outages. We were given plenty of warning that this could happen, and now it's proven to be so. Those who prepared are safe in their homes. The unprepared are trying to get what they need and are having a difficult time. For some, their work demands that they be out in this weather to feed livestock, restore power, and many other activities that are ongoing, regardless of weather. We appreciate all those who sacrifice their own comfort to keep America moving.

When we are warned, God gives us time to prepare. There are many warnings in God's Word. God is giving us time to prepare. Those things we are warned about will take place.

Are you prepared? There is time right now to prepare.

January 10

Inexcusable

Romans 2:1–11

Some believe that God accepts them just the way they are and that He will allow them to continue to live a life of sin and still be accepted by Him. I would challenge them to go to God's Word and read the first two chapters of Romans. The writer of Romans very clearly describes God's love and mercy but also God's divine judgment of sin and the life of one who lives in sin. This is not a decision that we make as individuals. This is God's decision, and this is truth!

Man tries to fit God into his own image. The truth is, God has made us in His own image. Our Creator extends to us marvelous, wonderful, and great mercy and grace. It is not what we deserve, but He gives it to us anyway. All we must do is accept it, receive it, and dwell in it.

January 11

Joy Equals Strength

Psalm 21:1

The King shall joy in thy strength O Lord. These words were part of a song the psalmist David sang to the Lord, and it has great value even today.

As we walk through life, there are days when we need God's strength and help. God's joy gives itself into our lives and becomes strength.

Paul, the apostle, shared these words with us: "I can do all things through Christ which strengtheneth me" (Philippians 4:13 AKJV). May God strengthen you today as you set out to accomplish what God has put before you.

January 12

Get Wisdom

Proverbs 1:1-6

To paraphrase one of the most insightful passages in Proverbs, *In all of your getting, get wisdom*. That verse has spoken to me many times and has proven to be a mainstay in my life. Wisdom will give you insight into your life beyond natural ability. Wisdom from God will provide stability and direction in a crazy, mixed-up world. Godly wisdom is needed and vital input in your daily life.

Yes, life is full of "getting," but in all that activity, getting wisdom is most important. Wisdom is a vital component in decision-making. It is a prime building component of character. Wisdom is an anchor in the turmoil of life situations. Sometimes it takes great effort to get wisdom, but it is well worth the effort.

January 13

Lord Rain Down on Me

Joel 2:23

A soaking rain and then a drenching rain—that is what we have had in our area in the last few days. We are thankful for the moisture. The rain reminds me of how God works in our lives. Sometimes He soaks us, giving us what we need in a gentle way. Other times, He pours Himself into our lives!

Enough rain fell that it filled up the ponds and reservoirs and spilled over into the environment, which filled up the next creek, pond, and reservoir. Enough rain falls from God that it fills up our lives and souls and spills over into the next individual. I love both events. There are times that I need the gentle filling. At other times, I need the drenching.

Lord God Almighty, let today be a day of drenching.

January 14

God Is for Us

Romans 8:31

In his letter to the Romans, Paul asks this question: "If God be for us, who can be against us?" Paul then shares with us that God even forsook His only Son for our sakes.

Yes, we may face opposition, calamity, or even death, but God will never abandon us. God is fully vested in our redemption, and He will not quit being there for those who are His in Christ Jesus.

My desire is to have God for me, not against me. I must do my part in accepting God's salvation through Jesus Christ, but when I do, that puts me in a right relationship with God.

God is for me. He wants to help me. He wants me. He wants you too.

January 15

Hard Road Transformed to Easy

Psalm 16:7–11

We sometimes look upon life's circumstances as a hard row to hoe or a hard road. Sometimes the hard road is transformed into the easy road. At times, we face things that we see as being extremely difficult, challenging, or unattainable. These can become much easier if we trust God to help us through it. God is willing, but we need to ask Him. The psalmist shares that God is always at our right hand. Talk about easy access—God makes Himself available!

Is there a difficult task ahead of you? Give it to God. Allow Him to do His part. The task before you will become much easier. Trust Him. Ask Him. He's right there beside you!

January 16

Cast All Your Care

1 Peter 5:7

For those carrying a heavy burden today, Jesus wants you to know that He's willing to pick up the burden for you. God's Word encourages us to cast all our cares upon Jesus because he cares for us. The word *cast* here is not a word suggesting gently laying our cares in Jesus's arms. It's strongly suggesting that we need to throw them into the arms of Jesus. Throw the burden with force! Throw that burden like you mean it. Get rid of it! Throw it in the arms of Jesus. If you are reluctant to throw it in the arms of Jesus, you may never be rid of the burden.

Jesus is waiting. Cast all your cares upon Him. Throw it with such force that it shakes your world. Forcibly get rid of them by casting all your cares upon Jesus. He cares for you.

January 17

How Do I Cast My Cares?

1 Peter 5:5–11

Jesus encourages us to cast our cares upon Him. The question arises: how do we cast upon Jesus something that has such a grip on our lives, souls, and spirits; something that there seems to be no way to be rid of? Our deepest desire is to be rid of it, but the grip of this life-controlling thing sticks to us like plastic that is full of static electricity. No matter how hard we try to get rid of it, it still clings to us.

I recognize the frustration, failed attempts, and futility of doing this repeatedly again and again. How can I be rid of this thing that grips me? The first step is to recognize my own failed attempts and recognize that I must have help—help that comes only from God. When I am at this point of recognition, I am at a point of receiving help from God. When I am at a point of laying down my messy life in the presence of the Holy God, with everything displayed before Him, I am at a place where God can begin to work.

Maybe I do not have the strength to throw my burden into Jesus's arms. Maybe all I am is a mess who is unable to do anything. When I ask for Jesus's help, He will scoop me up in His hands and shelter me in His arms. And as a potter would mold a piece of clay that has lumps and impurities in it, Jesus takes my life and begins to reshape it in the image and plan that He has for me.

Lay your heap of a mess at the feet of Jesus. Give all of yourself, your life, your mess, even your unwillingness to Jesus. He is the only one who can make something spectacular out of your mess.

January 18

Who Am I?

Psalm 8:4

Who is God that He would care for me? I am a mere human, made of dust, and prone to a sinful nature. I cannot force God to do anything or to like me. I have no power over God to make Him do any one thing, just for me. Yet God loves me, cares for me, and my companionship, and He even wants me. How can I love God the way that I do? It's because He first loved me.

Today, recognize that God loves you. He cares for you as though you were the only human created. His great love is beyond human comprehension. Let God love you today. You can't help but love Him back.

January 19

Human Sacrifice—An Ugly Epidemic

Leviticus 18:21

How does a nation, culture, and world repent of the sin of human sacrifice? At first glance, we would say of our nation that we do not have human sacrifice, as there are no ceremonies at religious gatherings where we tie up humans and sacrifice them before an imaginary god. But the reality is that human sacrifice is a worldwide epidemic in the form of legalized abortion of human life. I believe—and medical science not only supports but proves and validates—that human life begins at conception. In just a short time—just minutes after sperm has been deposited into a fertile environment—the union of a live female egg and live male sperm takes place, conception occurs, and a new life begins. To terminate this life is an abomination before God Almighty and places society in a place of wickedness before almighty God.

If you believe that abortion is a small problem, consider that worldwide, since 1973, there have been approximately 1.47 *billion* abortions. That is 19.5 percent—nearly one in five—of today's world population of 7.5 billion people. In the USA, approximately 59.78 million abortions have taken place since 1973, representing 18.3 percent of our current US population. Indeed, we have engaged in human sacrifice at a catastrophic level.

Repentance comes when we recognize that we have sinned and have gone against God with our wicked ways. Repentance places us before almighty God in a place of contrite hearts and brokenness before the giver of life, God Almighty. Repentance is turning away from the evil and wickedness, pursuing God and His righteousness, and realizing that human life is in His hands and not for us to take, just for our convenience. God gives life! Let's embrace His way and repent of our human sacrifice.

January 20

Turning a Test into a Testimony

1 Peter 1:7

A line from a favorite song of mine is, "Turn your test into a testimony." What a positive way to turn our tests into triumphs. Each of us faces our own tests throughout life. Life tests are sometimes extremely difficult, often lasting an unbearable time.

How we handle the test and how we allow God to help us turn it into a testimony is vital. God's Word promises that He will never leave us or forsake us. Sometimes in our testing, it may seem that God has abandoned us, but that is a lie from the deceiver of man, Satan himself. God's Word and His promises hold true no matter how the human heart feels or how the human mind comprehends. Even if the testing turns into tragedy, God can still create triumph out of tragedy.

If the test you are going through has broken you into pieces, let me encourage you to gather all the pieces and bring them to the feet of Jesus. One of Jesus's greatest abilities is to gather the brokenness and put it back together even better than it was before.

Let's make it a practice to allow God to turn our tests into testimonies!

January 21

What's Really in Your Heart?

2 Chronicles 32:31

What's really in your heart? In 2 Chronicles 32:31 (NLT), we find this about King Hezekiah: "However, when ambassadors arrived from Babylon to ask about the remarkable events that had taken place in the land, God withdrew from Hezekiah in order to test him and to see what was really in his heart."

I believe that God already knew what was in the king's heart, but God wanted Hezekiah to know his own heart. Sometimes the tests we go through are to reveal what is in our own hearts.

God is truly remarkable in that He gives each of us free will. The proof of our devotion to God is in the testing. What is really in your heart?

Lord God Almighty, may I pass the test, and may You find sincere and passionate devotion to You as I go through every test.

January 22

God Will Make A Way

1 Corinthians 10:13

So, things didn't go as planned! The plan now becomes a change in plans. We have all faced this situation in life. Plans change, and life changes. It seems that life is full of these changes. That which was going to be now becomes something different, and we must plan accordingly. Life is a mix of life-changing plans. But it's nothing to worry about! We serve and trust in the God who has known the plan since long before we were born. It was His plan all along, even though it seems like multiple changes to us.

I think God delights in making a way when there doesn't seem to be any plan at all. Let God work His plan in your life today. Life is an adventure! Look forward to it!

January 23

Doors Opened or Closed

Proverbs 8:34

Life's decisions are very easy when there is only one open door to walk through. It is much more difficult when there is more than one door, with maybe even some open windows, and the decision is entirely up to me. I have made decisions that proved wrong. At other times, when I have asked the Lord which door or window to choose, and I listened closely to Him and followed His guidance, things have worked well. Life is better when all things work well.

Lord, help me to seek Your instruction when faced with multiple open doors and windows. And when there is only one door, may I trust that You are the one who opened the door and have walked ahead of me, preparing my path.

January 24

Working Faith

James 2:18–26

God's Word says that faith without works is dead. That should indicate to us that faith with works brings about miracles!

Abraham believed God's promise that he would be the father of many nations. Abraham and Sarah, at the ages of one hundred and ninety, respectively, and with their bodies being as good as dead, acted upon God's promise. A baby was conceived, and many nations have been Abraham's inheritance since that time.

Job trusted God to the point of saying that even if God "slayed" him, he would still trust Him. His faith and trust in God brought him into a place of God's restoration, of blessings and prosperity in his life.

Peter did walk on water, but he had to first get out of the boat. John was given a vision of heaven, but he had to open his eyes. Sometimes faith is as simple as doing the normal everyday activities while believing that God will use them for His glory.

Perhaps your task is as simple as getting out of the boat. Perhaps it is to open your eyes for a great vision that God wants to place in your life.

Lord God Almighty, let our faith be full of works, and let our works be full of faith.

January 25

God First Loved Me

John 3:16

"That God should love a sinner such as I, how wonderful is love like this?" Those words are part of the first verse of one of the hymns of the church. We often marvel at why God would love us even before we were born. Furthermore, why would He love us after we are born, living the lives that we live? God is who He says is! God is love! You cannot fully explain God's love. It is often totally unexplainable.

I am so glad that God first loved me. With so much news about humanity's lack of love for the unborn, we need to stop and consider God's love for us. Whether planned or not, when we were conceived, God made provision for us. Not only did He make room for us, but He sent His only begotten Son, Jesus Christ, to die for us, that we might have salvation.

Love—it certainly is a God thing! And it's obvious that humanity lacks love. May God's love shine brighter through my life today.

January 26

God Walks with Us and Lifts Us Up

James 4:10

There are two distinct times that God has personally walked among men. The first was when God came down and walked with Adam and Eve in the garden of Eden. This was before sin entered the world. The second time was when Jesus, the Son of God, came to this world as a baby, grew up as a child, became an adult, and died as the supreme sacrifice for all our sins, all in the span of thirty-three years.

God's Holy Spirit does walk among humankind after the outpouring of his Holy Spirit on the day of Pentecost, shortly after Jesus's resurrection. God's plan as Father, Son, and Holy Spirit was to walk among us. As Christians, we rejoice in the fact that God chooses to walk among us in the person of His Holy Spirit.

The primary purpose of God's walking among humans was to draw them unto Him. As Christians, let us be careful that we do not try to draw God unto ourselves; rather, we should allow God to draw us to Him.

God's desire is to bring us up. Let's let God do what He desires to do. Let Him bring us up!

January 27

Worn Out from Ministry

Mark 6:30–32

As we begin to move toward a busy week, I am reminded of Jesus's life. He ministered until he was worn out physically and then went to a quiet place to rest and pray and prepare for the next time of ministry. Hard work is important, whether at your job or in the kingdom of God. I admire those who expend their energy in doing something completely, and at the end, they have nothing left to give and must rest and recharge their bodies. I am thankful for Jesus's example to us, and I want to be like Jesus. In a few short days, I will be with a team on the mission field in Peru, South America. I want to be one of those who, at the end of each day, is completely drained because I have poured my life into what I do. Wear yourself out for Jesus. It's a rewarding experience!

January 28

Hopefulness, Not Hopelessness

Psalm 16:1–11

When hopelessness overwhelms us, our God, who is hope, still stands where He has always been. When tragedy strikes, our God of peace and comfort still stands in His rightful place. When the questions without answers bombard our thinking, the God of all knowledge still sits on the throne. When the road ahead appears to be impassable, our God has already mapped out a way through because He is the way-maker. When sorrow consumes us and crushes our spirits, our God in heaven already stands, bearing our sorrow. When life is crushing down, and even taking a breath is painful, our God breathes life into our being. In everything that impacts physical and spiritual life here on earth, our God remains the same yesterday, today, and tomorrow and for all eternity.

January 29

Is There Anything Too Hard for God?

Jeremiah 32:17, 27

Can it be done? The circumstances and the world around us scream *no*, but then God steps into the picture (though He has never been out of the picture), takes control of the situation, and the impossible becomes possible.

As a human, it seems I am bent on holding on to something until it is a complete wreck before I give it to God. I am learning that giving it to God before it becomes a "circumstance" is good! God's Word promises that God will guide us and help us. I continue to learn that leaning on Jesus is an act of faith, trust, and confidence that is vital to my present and future needs.

Jesus, my life rests securely in Your hands as I lean upon You.

January 30

Today's Decisions

Proverbs 16:9

Today and every day, I have the luxury of making decisions. It is a God-given privilege to be allowed to do so. With God guiding and directing me, I can choose wisely. I have experience in not choosing wisely and when I look back, it is because I didn't ask for God's help, or I ignored His direction. Can you believe that with all of God's expertise, knowledge, wealth, and power, I would not ask for or would ignore His direction? That's the human nature.

Lord God Almighty, help me to seek You in every decision I make—today, tomorrow, this week, and for the rest of my life! Your ways are far better than my ways. I desire to follow Your ways.

January 31

God Communicates with Me

Isaiah 30:21

What an awesome time we live in—technology that allows instant communication almost anywhere in the world, including video and sound. What a way to send the message of the gospel of Jesus Christ out into the highways and byways. I am thankful that God has allowed me to experience and utilize this technology to communicate what He lays on my heart each day.

But I have a realization that God still communicates with us in the same as He has since creation. His Spirit speaks to our spirits—one on one, teaching us, directing our paths, and guiding our steps. Long before we had the type of communication that we admire today, we had God speaking to us, one on one, no matter where we were. Long before we had personal trainers, we had God teaching us. I am so thankful that God has time for me and for each one of us—personal time that is helpful and meaningful. His communication form far exceeds any of our technology—God speaking to us by His Spirit! God's ways are above human ways, any time, all the time.

February 1

Could Be the Day

1 Corinthians 15:51–58

We are living in exciting times! Generations living today have experienced some of the most profound historical events that have ever been recorded. We are watching biblical prophecy and history unfold in dramatic fashion.

I have heard many people say they wish they had been alive when Jesus walked this earth. I am glad that I'm alive today, in these last days, to watch as biblical prophecy unfolds before my eyes.

I was born four years after Israel became a nation. I was in high school during the 1967 Middle East war. I have watched as Jerusalem has been returned to the ones to whom it has belonged ever since God gave that land to the Israelites. I am living amid the "great falling away" of the church, which the Bible says will happen in the last days. I am also living in the middle of a great revival that God is pouring out upon the world. Modern technology provides me with a front-row seat to watch and discover what God is doing on the earth.

God tells us in His Word that He will put a hook in the mouths of the enemies of Israel and draw them to Israel, as part of His plan to place His judgment upon them. We are living in the day that this is happening.

God has promised to come for His people, and He will fulfill that promise. This may be the day! Are you ready?

February 2

God Is Speaking to You!

1 Kings 19:9–13

What does it take to move an individual toward God? What does it take to move a nation or a culture toward God? It is true that God speaks to individuals in a still, small voice, inviting them to draw close to Him, but it is obvious that a multitude of humanity is not listening?

Sudden disaster often pushes us toward God for a brief time, and we acknowledge that we need God's help, but as time passes, we return to our old way of life, ignoring God and His still, small voice.

Today, recognize that God desires to draw you unto Him. Don't wait for a disaster to turn to Him. Hear His still, small voice as He speaks to you in the quiet of your heart. Let yourself be drawn to your Creator. Life is so much better when you yield to God.

February 3

Full and Overflowing

Psalm 16:11

God made each one of us different, but He also made each one of us alike! Each of us has unique features, personality, looks, and more, but each human heart has a place within it that nothing can fill but God Himself. Individuals have tried to fill that place with everything but God, only to find that they become emptier and more desperate for the one—the only one—who can fill that void.

I have only to look closely at those I meet today and pray that God, by His Spirit, will reveal the fullness or emptiness of their hearts. There is no satisfaction with emptiness, but there is complete satisfaction with God's fullness. God is willing to fill that place in you that is reserved only for Him.

> May God's Holy Spirit begin to soften your heart and make you receptive to His fullness.
>
> May I be ready to point hearts to the one who can satisfy and bring fullness.

February 4

Lost and Hopeless

Psalm 39:7–8

As I drove through the streets of Lima, Peru, well after midnight, I noticed a significant number of people walking the streets. Yes, it was a beautiful evening, but I was struck by the hopelessness that was evident in their walks and demeanors. I would categorize many of whom I saw as lost and without hope.

Finding people who are lost and without hope—that is why we are here for the few hours our team will be in Lima, and tomorrow, on into the jungle. Our world, whether here or at home, is filled with lost, hopeless, hurting people who need Jesus. While we're here these few days, many will look at our team members, wishing they could have what we have.

May they see Jesus more than they see our ability to pay for meals and gifts. May they see the Savior of the world evident in our lives, more than they see anything else.

February 5

Biblically Correct

Psalm 119:105–106

There is so much "correctness" placed on society today that most people are afraid to voice their thoughts or express their beliefs. There is political correctness, as well as cultural, ethnic, lifestyle, religious, and many more "correctness" demands placed on our culture. I contend, argue, challenge, and am persuaded that "biblical correctness" supersedes any and all other correctness. If I am biblically correct, I am correct in all other areas, regardless of cultural views. I choose to be biblically correct, using God's Word as the standard for how I should conduct life.

Lord God, help me to stand on Your Word, speak Your Word, and live Your Word. Let me be an example of a correct "correctness"—biblical correctness.

February 6

God's Handiwork

Psalm 19:1

The view from below is quite different from the view from above. A couple of days ago, I had a view from thirty-five thousand feet. Today, my view is at ground level.

I can't physically see God, but I can certainly see His handiwork. God's influence is in all of creation. I encourage you to observe the very small things of nature for a little while today. Look closely so that you can see how God has intricately created even the smallest detail into His creation. If He cares enough about that, He cares much more for you and me.

Enjoy His care!

February 7

What's My Full Potential?

James 1:1–8

Often, someone's or something's full potential is hidden deep within, and in order to utilize that full potential, it must be drawn out. I believe that within those who serve God, God Himself is drawing out potential that those people cannot see.

Many times, it is not that we have natural ability or talent, but rather that God takes our availability and then gives us ability. It's the same with wisdom. In our own wisdom, we often fail, but if we ask God, His wisdom is not only right but perfect. Wise counsel says to seek God's wisdom. In doing so, the potential that God wants to expose in us will be drawn out. Ask God for wisdom. It is wise to do so.

February 8

Weary and Susceptible

Psalm 2:1–6

Sometimes the body is weary, and the mind is slow, especially after a very long day of meetings, flights, and very-late-night driving to get home. I find that I am more susceptible to attack from the enemy of my soul when I have had such a day. It's easy to think that evil is overwhelming, and godliness is absent when we're bone-tired and weary.

I believe that David experienced those kinds of days as he fled from King Saul. David knew that God was with him and protected him, but it was easy to think that the enemy was winning the battle. The Lord my God is a very present help, not just in times of trouble but always—and probably more so when I am bone-tired and weary! Thank you for Your presence, Lord God Almighty!

February 9

I Want to Be Like—Jesus

1 Peter 4:21–25

When I grow up, I want to be like … Even as a grandfather, I find myself occasionally thinking those thoughts. All of us have met people who inspire us and motivate us and who are mentors who lead us. Those individuals are great teachers, leaders, and motivators, regardless of their occupations or positions in life.

There are plenty of examples of who I *don't* want to be like, and I find if I dwell on those thoughts too long, I become more like those who I don't want to be like. Finding a good example and desiring to become like that person is an admirable quality and a worthwhile endeavor. But there is someone better to pattern our lives after.

God's Word gives us instruction to pattern our lives after Jesus—He is a flawless example. People, on the other hand, even those we want to pattern our lives after, are flawed and imperfect. Yep, when I grow up, I want to be like Jesus!

February 10

A Treasure from God

Proverbs 31:10

The greatest gift God has given to me besides His wonderful salvation is a godly wife. It all started when we were in high school, and God brought her to visit the church I attended. He allowed her to walk past me and then sit down in front of me. Even as a teenager, she was full of grace and walked with confidence—and wow, how beautiful God had created her. I can still picture in my mind those steps she took while in my view. I was captivated, hooked, and caught all in those moments when I first saw her. When people ask how we met, I often tell them that I liked what I saw, and I have been chasing her ever since!

God had carefully orchestrated that visit (in itself a long story for another time). I cannot tell you what the Sunday school lesson was on that day, I can't tell you which songs we sung, and I can't tell you what the message was about, but I can tell you that my eyes were fastened onto this beautiful young lady and have been ever since. That was over fifty years ago, and I still love looking at her and thinking those same thoughts as when I first saw her. Me? Well, I was just a face in a maze of other faces, all new to her, but with time, God allowed her to see me (finally), fall in love with me, and make my dreams come true! I am in love with God's gift, and yes, I am still chasing her!

Happy birthday, LaDonna.

February 11

Ruts or a Smooth Path?

Proverbs 3:1–6

We lived about fifteen miles out in the country while I was growing up. The last five miles were dirt roads, and every time it rained, those roads became a quagmire of mud. Often folks would get stuck and would have to get a tractor to pull them out. Sometimes the vehicle would get crossways in the road, and we would spend much time backing up and going forward, trying to straighten out the vehicle. Many times, the vehicle would have to make dozens of tries to get back on course. We always felt fortunate to make it home without getting stuck.

Whoever was the first one to travel the road after a rain was able to choose the best path and make a "rut" for others to follow. If the first one chose wrong, the car would either get crossways in the road or wind up in the ditch and need to be pulled out. The next vehicle coming along would likely fall into the rut and follow the same path as the first vehicle, even getting crossways in the road.

The roads have been surfaced with shale since then and are not nearly as bad when it rains, and I am thankful for the improvement. The path that you and I are on in life is like what I have described here. Often we are in a rut, following someone else's attempt to drive a course that will take the person to his or her destination, or we are traveling on an untraveled road. God wants to put us, as individuals, on an untraveled road, and He does not want us to be susceptible to the ruts formed by the previous traveler. Ruts—they are not what I want to follow! I want to follow Jesus on a path free from ruts.

February 12

Spiraling Wickedness

2 Timothy 3:1–9

Our world continues its dizzy spiral into wickedness and acts of violence in the name of something that promotes death of nonfollowers. Simple fix: Jesus Christ living in the lives of people of all nations, cultures, and people groups. When that happens, there is no need for hate, vengeance, or violent killing. No need for sin indulgence, and no need to take the lives of innocent people. The world and its inhabitants need Jesus living in their hearts. God is love, but when He is not invited into our hearts, wickedness fills the void.

I have no place to judge the individual, but I have an obligation to judge the act! I judge the action of the fifty murders in Orlando as an act of wickedness. Only Jesus can change the heart of an individual. Only Jesus's love can change the wicked intent of sinful man. Our world needs Jesus and what He can do in each of our lives.

February 13

Epic Fail

Proverbs 15:22

It's apparent that all humankind's attempts to stop the violence in the world are failing miserably. That is the true nature of humankind's plans—they fail! Epic fail! We must wake up to the fact that the more humankind tries to fix its problems, the worse the problems get. Just take a quick look at any social problem people have tried to fix. There has been failure on nearly every hand, and if money was spent on it, that usually fell into the wrong hands.

God has a plan! It is a perfect plan—flawless and achievable. I suggest we bypass humankind's attempt and incorporate God's plan. God's plans are unfailing.

Lord God Almighty, give us wisdom to know and follow Your plans for our lives, our culture, and our world.

February 14

Hate Leads to Violence

Proverbs 10:12

Violence is violence! Perhaps the worst violence is not gun violence or mob violence but hatred. No gun has ever gotten up from its place of safety on its own and committed violence. Hate causes individuals to commit violence, with or without a gun or other weapon in their hands. How many times in recent history have masses of people been moved to violence because of explosive words of hate? Hate is the go-to language of the world today. Jesus admonishes us to *love* those that hate us. From my viewpoint, there are a lot of folks to love in this world today. Hate is everywhere. What an opportunity for the love of God to be on display.

February 15

My Identification

1 Peter 2:1–10

I do a lot of traveling on my job. I spent last night in Paris—Paris, Texas. LaDonna and I have been to both Paris, France, and Paris, Texas, and there is a world of difference. When I just said that I was in Paris, you might have placed me in France in your mind, enjoying the scenery and culture there. Instead, I am enjoying the scenery and culture of northeast Texas. Word identification is something that can catch us off guard. Christian—a name or an identification? We supposedly live in a Christian nation, but many would say that is in name only. A majority of the people are not living as Christians.

May Jesus so live through me that anyone who sees me can easily identify me as Christian. Let the people of God—Christians—live and walk as those worthy of carrying the name *Christian*.

February 16

My Eternal Home

Revelation 21:1–4

Tonight, I plan to be home to enjoy the comforts that await me there. There really is no place like home, even after you have visited Paris (Texas). Home! I belong there, and I am accepted and welcomed there. After this long journey, it simply will be good to be home.

I'm also on a journey to my eternal home. The journey is sometimes long and hard, but the welcome that awaits me is beyond description. The provisions of the comforts of my home here on earth will pale in comparison to what awaits me in heaven. That's the home that I'm waiting for. Each day brings me closer to that eternal home. Each day of travel this week brought me closer to my being home this weekend.

I am thankful for life's journey and those I meet along the way. Heading home—it's a wonderful thing!

February 17

That Heavenly Reunion

1 Thessalonians 4:13–18

Our home is filled with family from distant parts of the country. They have come to celebrate the life of my brother's father-in-law. Once again, stories of life abound. Each person has an abundance of different stories, and it's wonderful to hear them!

Heaven will be a place of meeting those who have gone before us. I can't wait to hear all the stories! I know that I will want to spend time with Jesus, but I also have a yearning to see all those who are there and hear them tell their stories.

These next several days will be story time for my sister-in-law's family. Let the stories begin, and if I've heard them before, I don't mind hearing them again.

Sunday is coming, and I can't wait to hear the stories of Jesus. Yes, tell me the story of Jesus!

February 18

God's Word Is Clearly Descriptive

John 14:1–6

I love descriptive phrases such as "I'm in a pickle," or "I'm in a jam." (Must be a large pickle, and I wonder if it's strawberry jam.) I can just see someone "in a fix" being used to fix a leaking water pipe. While most of us know what is meant when we hear those phrases, I still delight in picturing what was vocalized with the word choices.

God's Word is straightforward and often paints a clear picture of what was said. When Jesus said that the path to heaven was straight and narrow, He was not describing a winding, hilly, scenic route. When Jesus said, "I am the way, the truth, and the life," He was not talking about one of many ways. Jesus was talking about *the* way—reading God's Word! It is clearly what He meant, and He speaks clearly to us.

February 19

The Value of Your Name

Proverbs 22:1–2

Often, there is considerable value in a name. Imagine two paintings, side by side. Both would look good on the living room wall, but the one signed by Van Gogh is far more valuable than the other. Name brands are considered higher value than store brands, and American-made is superior to foreign-made products.

Being called a Christian must never be lumped together with all the other religions that are named or unnamed. The value of being called a Christian must be significantly higher than being called by any other name. The value is not just in the name, though. It is in the quality of the performance. Genuine *Christian* demonstrates superiority over any other in how we, as Christians, live in surrender to God Almighty. If we are Christians, then let's demonstrate the true value that's within us. Jesus in our hearts and lives—that's valuable!

February 20

Truth Builds Character

Psalm 15:1–5

I was told that someone had lied to me. The sad part is that this news did not surprise me. I had questioned this individual's integrity before, but this confirmation of the lack of integrity will make me question this individual's every action and statement. Integrity tells the truth, even when it hurts. I know full well the value of confidentiality and the holding of privileged information until a proper time to share it. Lying to cover what is a confidential matter is never a good thing.

Some people resort to lies to cover true feelings and business relationships. Unfortunately, the telling of untruths has become a way of life for many. My observation of those I know to have this problem is that they are miserable in life, soul, and spirit.

God Almighty, help me to be a man of integrity, one who tells the truth. Help those who tend to be untruthful to understand that truth will set them free.

February 21

It's a Generational Thing

Psalm 145:3–7

I completed my sixth mission trip to the jungle of Peru in early 2017. Since my first experience, I have wondered each time how the current trip can top the last one, yet each time, God has ordained a new and invigorating experience that exceeds previous visits. I asked several of those who made this year's trip what their personal highlight was, and I was intrigued with the varied responses from veterans and first-timers. While every segment is a highlight, there usually are one or two that stand out—at least a little. For me, it was a visit to the jungle churches of Nauta, Mira Flores, and San Jose de Sisa and hearing my oldest son share his testimony with the people of the jungle. We are two generations of sharing the good news of the gospel to the people of the jungle of Peru!

Next year, I am planning to take a member of the third generation of my family to Peru. Only God could orchestrate something as elaborate as this. I am already looking forward to our being back in the Peruvian jungle. (Get ready. Peru! Third generation getting ready to experience your culture and serve you!)

We are already excited, and it is still fifty weeks away! Other members of the third generation have asked when will it be their turn. I love that they want to experience what God is doing in the jungle of Peru.

Three generations experiencing God's move in the Peruvian jungle—I can't wait!

February 22

Tedious Work

Esther 8:13

One of our stops last week while we were in Lima, Peru, was the Francisco Church. The library contained over twenty thousand books handwritten in the fifteenth and sixteenth centuries. Volumes of carefully written books lined the shelves, and it gave me a feeling of awe to consider the effort that went into creating them.

Handwritten music was displayed on a rotating lectern that was large enough for the whole choir to see. The ability to create these pieces was a God-given talent. And now, hundreds of years later, it was on display for us to view.

You may think that your work in God's kingdom is tedious, boring, trivial, unexciting, or time-consuming, but some future day, someone may look at your work and contemplate your talent, passion, zeal, and time spent in what you contributed to the kingdom of God. Whatever you do, do it as unto the Lord. Make it as perfect as possible. After all, God is watching.

February 23

Mentoring a Younger Generation

Proverbs 4:1–13

It has been my privilege this week to travel with an intern who is working for our company this year. She still has one year of college left but is investigating opportunities that will exist after graduation. Of all the things that go wrong in our culture today, this intern has it all right—intelligence, common sense, receiving mentorship, open to new opportunities, and a pleasant demeanor. Her God-given abilities and talent are on display, along with a humble attitude. A. B. will be successful in whatever field she chooses.

I am thrilled when I see those in our younger generation excel in life and in their work. I am thankful to God that there are still young people who were raised properly and who have become amazing individuals. This advice from God's Word stands out. In all your getting, get wisdom. Young person, with God's help, you can excel, and I encourage you to do so.

February 24

Investing in Others

Psalm 1:1–6

The value of investing in someone else's life is not fully known until later. Whether in a person's personal or business life, investing takes time and effort. As I look back over the years to business relationships in which I have invested, I am humbled by the influence I had in their lives. It was not so much me as it was God's living through me and just being an example to them of what I felt my responsibilities should be. I treated them fairly and with respect and provided a pattern to follow. At the time, I had no idea of the impact I was making. I was humbled that God would direct my path in such a way.

We also have an opportunity to invest in the lives of those with whom we attend church. Doing so can be an important step in someone's life. Investing in others—it's worth it.

February 25

Living through Trials

James 1:12

Trouble and trials are a part of the life we live while on earth. A songwriter penned these words: "It will be worth it all when we see Jesus." Going through a trial can be very difficult, and we look forward to coming through it and putting it behind us.

But when we meet Jesus as our Savior in heaven for the very first time, *all* trials will be over. The race will have been run, and a victor's crown will be ours! Unfortunately, there will be those who have not accepted Jesus as Savior. According to God's holy Word, their earthly trials will pale in comparison to their eternal trouble and trial of eternal torment, pain, and suffering.

For Christians, there may be trials today, but there is hope for tomorrow and a knowledge that when we see Jesus, the trials of this life are will be over! Living today is worth it, knowing the hope of tomorrow. Jesus—He is our steadfast hope!

February 26

Accountability—A Culture in Need

Galatians 6:1–10

Corruption and its acceptance are splashing over our headlines again today. It has become the new normal to see how much people can involve themselves in vile deeds and not be held accountable. And in a nation that is made of people by the people, we stand idly by, allowing it to happen on a larger scale and on a more frequent basis.

Godly people must not only believe in God's standards but must also hold those who represent us accountable for holding and adhering to those standards. I believe in mercy and grace, as I have been the recipient of those gifts many times in my life. But along with those gifts came an understanding that I needed to repent, turn from sin and reject sinful desires and go in a different direction, and not try to get by with more the next time. For most folks in the headlines today, there is no indication of repentance, just a desire to do more and do it more often.

Almighty God, we need Your help, and we need to be a people worthy of the blessing of democracy that You have allowed us to have.

February 27

Repetitive Sin

Hebrews 10:26–27

The Old Testament book of Amos contains the promises of God to send complete destruction by fire to cities, cultures, and nations, not because of their single sin but because of repeated sin, knowing all the while that God was displeased. Repeated sin—what a tragedy! We know that it is sin because of God's Word, yet we got away with it before, so we are enticed to do it again until it becomes a lifestyle. A lifestyle of repeated sin invites God's judgment, whether individually, cooperatively, culturally, or as a nation or world. Our world is full of wicked sin. Only by God's mercy have we been spared God's judgment. Repentance and following hard after God is the only way that we will not face judgment for repeated sin.

Lord God Almighty, keep us from sin that so easily besets us.

February 28

Deceived

1 John 3:4–10

Human injury and death have been inflicted through the actions of humans using any object that they can pick up and use as a weapon. Willfully violent acts of humankind cannot be blamed on those inanimate objects. Almost always, human will initiates such destructive force. God's Word declares that the enemy of our souls comes to kill and destroy, and so human will desires to destroy life at any cost is directed by the deceiver, Satan himself. Weapons of any sort—poison, drugs, rope, rocks, knives, guns—cannot act on their own.

Our world wants to blame anything and everything but the human will and the deceiver of our souls. Humankind must be accountable for its actions. Placing blame on inanimate objects has not one shred of validity. People—some who call themselves Christian—are being deceived into placing misdirected blame onto something, often inanimate, other than where true blame should be placed.

Lord God Almighty, grant to Your followers true discernment of how the enemy of our souls is deceiving those around us with lies. Help us to have wisdom to challenge misdirected blame and to place blame on the real culprit. Satan, you are a liar, and the truth is not in you! God, You alone are truth!

February 29

Additional Time

2 Peter 3:8

I have good news to pass along, especially if you are like me and have put off doing some things until later in the year. First, 2020 is a leap year. Each of us has one full extra day this year—twenty-four hours, or 1440 minutes, or 86,400 seconds. This extra day is a gift our world gives to us by being about a quarter of a day slower than 365 days revolving around the sun. Every four years we get to add one day to the calendar. One day! That's 0.27 percent of the entire year. Doesn't seem like much, but just look what can be accomplished in one day.

In 2016—also a leap year—we added one second to the last minute of the year. This was because the earth's rotation is not precisely twenty-four hours. That officially made 2016 the longest year in recent history—366 days plus one second. Don't waste the extra day this year!

Gods handiwork is amazing. That this globe on which we live has been spinning and revolving around our sun since creation, and with our precision timepieces, we have only to add one second every eighteen months. God is amazing, and He amazes me every day.

March 1

It's a Priority

John 6:40

Priorities change over time. Some things that were top priorities some forty years ago have lost their importance, and different things now have top priority. Life is full of changing priorities, but the topmost priority in my life has always been my relationship with Jesus Christ. God says of Himself that He changes not. If He was my top priority then, He must be my top priority now and for the rest of my life. Other priorities change, but my relationship with God the Father, Son, and Holy Spirit is still top priority. Make Him number one in your life. It's the best decision you will ever make.

March 2

Excitement as Heaven Prepares for Our Arrival

1 Thessalonians 4:13–18

I sense there must be excitement in heaven as this earthly world rushes headlong toward its appointed destiny. God says that this world will be purified by fire, but before that happens, God has promised that He will call His church, the bride of Jesus Christ, to be with Him forever in heaven. I have experienced long waits in people laden lines for mass-transit transportation, just to board an airplane, but just for a moment, let's imagine the volume of people that will make this trip to heaven. God's Word declares that "in the twinkling of an eye"—less than a single second of time—the dead in Christ will rise first, and then we who are living will be caught up to meet Jesus in the sky! Now that's a mass transit system I want to experience. I'm waiting for my ride. Come, Lord Jesus!

March 3

Seasons of Life

Ecclesiastes 3:1–8

I love the cycles of the seeding year that my job encounters. I live in and serve a region that has two distinct planting seasons for alfalfa. The spring planting season occurs during a very busy time, when all other spring crops are also planted. The late-summer seeding of alfalfa occurs after wheat harvest and before the fall crops are ready to harvest. It is the late-summer seeding period I like best because growers can concentrate on just seeding alfalfa without the concerns of getting other crops planted.

Certain seasons in our lives also are very full, but we must find the time and energy to read God's Word and spend time with God in prayer. During other life seasons, there is plenty of time to do so. I love those times when I'm not hurried by life.

If you are in a busy season of life, just make it a priority to read God's Word and spend time with Him. If you are in a not-so-busy season, enjoy the open time to be with God!

March 4

Hate Is Not God's Way

Proverbs 10:11–12

It's obvious that our world has enough hate; it is overflowing into our streets in the form of violence and destruction. What gain is there for an individual or faction to hate to this point? In many cases, the only "gain" is their own deaths. Their innocent family members must suffer the stigma of the actions of the perpetrator. There will be no pride in those violent actions; rather, the family members will carry the shame for the rest of their lives.

Jesus died, but He didn't kill others while being put to death. He died so that any of us who believe in Him will live and have life abundant! Those who are led to kill and destroy certainly do not exhibit any of the qualities of God that He places into man when he receives abundant life.

Lord God Almighty, I want an abundant life, not one of hate and destruction.

March 5

God's Standard of Integrity

Proverbs 11:3

Integrity is a choice, day by day as well as moment by moment. The lack of integrity is also a choice that puts one on a slippery slope to failure. Choose wisely, my friend! Our world is full of successful failures whose lack of integrity forces them to add lying, cheating, and corruption to their already sick lives. Unfortunately, they often make it look so attractive that others jump onto the slippery slope with them.

Integrity is one of God's standards. Where there is no integrity, there is no desire to please God, and where there is no desire to please God, there is devastation. Our world is full of devastation! Let men and women of integrity arise in our culture. Let them be examples to the world around them of what it looks like and what it means to live a life of integrity.

March 6

Improvement Is God's Plan for Us

2 Peter 1:1–11

Improving upon what we already have is an important part of success. Our world today seems bent on tearing down and destroying, rather than improving. Yesterday, I looked at varieties of alfalfa that have shown dramatic improvement over earlier varieties—not just your incremental improvement but head-and-shoulders-above-the-rest improvement. The breeders could have left the earlier product in place and moved on to other things, but they chose to stay the course and found ways and technology to greatly improve upon what was already there.

God is not ready to set you aside and move on to someone else. He still desires to introduce improvements into your life and make you head-and-shoulders better than what you were! I'm glad that God is still working on me.

March 7

Follow the Right Leader

Mark 8:34-38

What if the world around us followed God's Word like it was following the instructions of Pokémon GO? In my travels in 2016, I noticed a phenomenon of people walking about aimlessly, staring at their electronic device, intent on being one with it. Some even walked into traffic or fell off ledges because they were not paying attention to their surroundings. I have only observed the results of those participating in Pokémon GO but have never played along. I enjoy wholesome and fun-filled games and certainly am not against participation in them. This, though, reminds me of the story of the Pied Piper. From my observation, Pokémon GO is not leading people to heaven. Only Jesus can lead us in a manner that is pleasing to God. If you desire to participate in the most exciting game known to man, follow Jesus. Game on!

March 8

His Destruction Is Sure

Revelation 20:1-10

The enemy of our soul, Satan himself, is a defeated enemy. Though he has been given the ability to wreak havoc, destruction, and death upon this earth for a time, that time is limited. The end of Satan's abilities are clearly outlined in God's Word. God Almighty has the last word!

While living on earth as humans, we serve either God Almighty or Satan. Those who are not serving God at the end of their lives will receive the same demise as the enemy of our souls, Satan. The eternal judgment of God Almighty is final! There will be no escape, no mercy, no relief, and no friends.

Your friends may go to hell, and you may think they will have time together in friendship, but an eternal life of torment does not allow for the comfort of friends. Those in hell will be alone in their eternal torment, all because they didn't choose to serve God. What a tragedy.

There are eternal consequences that will affect you personally. Choose to serve God—that is the wise choice.

March 9

Fuel for the Fire

1 Corinthians 3:10–17

March 2017—the Plains of the United States are on fire! Tens of thousands of acres have burned, and multiple homes and buildings are completely lost. Communities and parts of cities are being evacuated as fire races before mighty winds that blow where they want. High air temperatures, extremely low humidity, dry vegetation, and powerful winds quickly explode even a small spark into horrendous destruction. Also contributing to the problem is that there is a tremendous amount of fuel just perfect for combustion.

Last year, there was abundant rainfall. Grass was lush and green and grew tall. Not all of it was consumed by cattle grazing or haying, and many fields had plenty of residue left from last year's harvest. The remaining vegetation died back last year as it matured or was frozen back by winter's temperatures. The fuel that remained was completely dry and perfect for wildfires. When the fire has passed, only bare ground and basement foundations will remain.

God's Word shares how fire is used to purify and to refine. God also tells us that one future day, this entire world will be burned completely, a final refinement and purification. In no way am I saying that the fires today are punishment from God on those who have lost homes, buildings, livestock, and fencing to the fires. The lesson here is to not let that with which God has blessed our lives dry up and become fuel for a wildfire. I want to use what God has blessed me with in building the kingdom of God today. Use me up today, Lord! I don't want anything left over for a fire to destroy tomorrow.

March 10

Fire—the Trial of Faith

1 Peter 1:7

We are grateful to those who have given selflessly of themselves to battle the wildfires that have swept the Plains. Firefighters, first responders, paramedics, and volunteers have joined together, forgoing sleep and rest to battle the flames. The largest fire has consumed over one-half million acres and is only partially contained. Many homes and outbuildings have been destroyed, along with thousands of head of livestock and innumerable wildlife. The cattle simply could not outrun the fire. In what is being referred to as the worst outbreak of wildfires in history, our part of the world is suffering tremendous loss. Fortunately, human loss of life remains low, thanks to evacuation and concentration on saving lives. Losing everything but your life is a profound place to be.

Last year, our son and his family lost everything but their lives to a wildfire near Hutchinson, Kansas. They have started rebuilding their lives, but the reality of losing everything has been hard to absorb. But they have their lives, and we are thankful.

God's Word shares with us that some will make it to heaven with just their souls with no reward following. The picture given is one who escapes the fire—but just barely and only with his or her soul. Personal loss of tangible things is hard! If those tangible things are the only thing I have, then I am very poor. God says for us to lay up treasure in heaven, where nothing can destroy it. The reality is that some have lost every tangible thing they had here on earth but escaped with their lives. I want to have some treasure under my name in heaven if I must face losing everything here on earth. Treasure in heaven—I am rich beyond measure.

March 11

Generous Giving

2 Corinthians 9:6–8

Generosity and kindness were evident yesterday as my travels took me to southwest Kansas and into the heart of some of the area's premier alfalfa production. Fires have devastated some two million acres of pasture, rangeland, and field residue in the Plains this week. Many thousands of head of livestock have been killed by the fast-moving fires, and many more that escaped have nothing to eat because feed supplies were also totally consumed by the fires. Generosity and kindness hit the roads immediately, as growers who had hay stocks began to load trucks and ship to those in need.

In yesterday's travels, I saw many loads of hay traveling toward the devastated area. Several states lifted bans on oversized/over-width loads of round bales for ease of delivery into the area. Those who are shipping, for the most part, are doing so without promise of being paid. Each load represents some two thousand to four thousand dollars, depending on the quality, plus fuel and driver time in shipping.

I enjoy stopping at the Love's fuel stations, and I understand they have offered to provide free fuel to those shipping livestock feed and farm supplies into the devastated areas. That is just how the generosity and kindness of US agriculture is manifested by our growers and suppliers. We did not need for Congress to take six months to develop a costly plan or to wait for a subsidy to be placed.

We saw a need and we responded! Generosity and kindness are never out of place. Thank you, American agriculture, for being generous and kind. You are storing up treasure in heaven!

March 12

Pressing In for the Win

Philippians 3:14

"March Madness" is running wild in the United States. It's a time when college basketball teams play for the title of best in the nation. There are two goals with backboards, one on each end of the court. Each is the same size, same height, and same diameter hoop. Each team defends one goal and uses the other to score points. The idea is to toss an official-size basketball through the hoop, scoring points for your team. Much is said about percentages of goals versus shots taken, and generally teams must have percentages higher than 50 percent to win the game.

Last night, as I watched a favorite team play, I observed that the ball continually missed the goal, and most of the time it landed in the hands of the opponent, then giving the opposing side the opportunity to score at the opposite end of the court. Last night, missing the mark (goal) was costly. The game was lost, in part, because the team missed the mark by a significant percentage.

When we miss the mark in the Christian life, just as in a ball game, there are serious consequences. Practice, practice, practice—that's what improves the ability to hit the mark. In practicing my Christian walk, I have missed many goals, but I am still in the game and striving to make each shot count. Lord God Almighty, help me as I continue practicing my position in Your kingdom today

Unforgettable Light and Laser Show

Revelation 4:5

Our journey this week has taken LaDonna and me to one of our favorite places—Branson, Missouri. It is spring break, and the city is full of families shivering in the cold as they involve themselves in their favorite activities. Ours is attending Praise Fest during the last half of the week, and prior to that, seeing *Moses* and a couple of other favorite musical shows. Last night's show was one of the most awesome light and laser shows we have ever witnessed. It was a thrilling experience as we watched the program unfold with flawless precision.

There is a light and sound show that I want to attend soon. John the Revelator describes this show in the throne room of God Almighty, as lightning and thunder go out from this room. I have experienced God's natural light shows here on earth, as lightning has struck very close by as I watched. I have watched the sky light up at dawn and dusk, and I have watched the spectacular creations of man, but nothing can compare to my anticipation of being in the presence of God Almighty and the light show that proceeds from God's throne room. I have purchased my ticket—or should I say that Jesus has purchased my ticket—to heaven to see this grand show. I dare say getting a ticket will be well worth the effort. Don't miss this experience of a lifetime.

March 14

Crossing Your Red Sea

Proverbs 3:5–6

I have experienced the crossing of the Red Sea twice in my life—once, several years ago, at Universal Studios in Hollywood, and again last night at the Sight and Sound Theater in Branson, Missouri. Modern technology has really enhanced the experience of today. Can you imagine a wall of water—perhaps over six hundred feet high, by some estimates—surrounding you and the people of Israel as you crossed the sea on dry ground? I find myself too many times underestimating what God can do. My little problems pale in comparison to what the children of Israel needed. God came through with great victory.

This year can be a great and complete victory in our lives! We may think we are backed into a corner with no way of escape, that we either will be overwhelmed by the enemy or drown. That's where the Israelites were. But God had a plan. God *always* has a plan. Even in the worst of situations and with way out, God has a plan. Trust fully in God and watch Him perform miracles. God can and will do it—today!

March 15

Music That Ministers

Psalm 150:1–5

Praise Fest 2017 in Branson concludes today. LaDonna and I have enjoyed the music, atmosphere, and ministry of this kind of music. Every lyric tells someone's story, and a catchy melody enhances the message. The hymn writer writes these words: "I love to tell the story." The truth is we have ignored the story for the sake of time and involvement in other things. The story—your story—needs to be told. If you are able to put it in prose form, that is awesome. For some, writing it down in normal conversational language is the way to go. For others, just verbalizing their stories to others is the best method. Whichever method you choose, tell your story. God has given each of us great answers to prayers during our lifetimes. Someone today needs to hear your story. Just tell it.

March 16

Music to Soothe the Soul

1 Samuel 16:23

I am reminded of the healing power of music. In God's Word, we find that King Saul invited David to play music for him when he was tormented, and David played until the tormenting spirit would leave. Paul and Silas had been beaten and then placed in stocks in the lower part of the prison, but around midnight, they lifted their voices in music, and God released them from that prison with a prison-shattering earthquake.

Music, done right, soothes the soul and lifts the spirit. Unfortunately, the world listens to a lot of music that does not fit into the soothing, uplifting category. I can only observe that restlessness, sinful thoughts, and godless influence are often identified with these other types of music. I desire that the music I listen to will invite the presence of a holy God into my life. My God soothes the soul and shatters my prisons.

March 17

God Speaks

Ezekiel 12:23a

The Old Testament books of Ezekiel and Jeremiah record several times the following phrases:

- "I the Lord have spoken it." (Ezekiel 24:14 AKJV)
- "The Lord of Heaven's Armies has spoken." (Isaiah 14:27 AKJV)
- "I the Sovereign Lord have spoken." (Ezekiel 12:28 NLT)

God was disclosing to Jeremiah His displeasure with Israel for replacing the sovereign God with the gods of the wicked nations around them and the impending destruction that God was going to bring upon them. The disasters that God promised did occur, and Israel was severely punished for their sin. In God's Word, God speaks clearly of blessing or judgment. There is no middle ground for you and me. He speaks judgment when we fail to follow Him and serve Him as sovereign God. He speaks blessing when we are fully committed to serving Him and have His Son Jesus living in our hearts.

Child of God, God has spoken! His words, found on the pages of scripture, are absolute and true. That which He has promised, He will fulfill. It is His Word!

"I the Sovereign Lord have spoken. (AKJV)" Be encouraged with God's spoken Word today.

Ready to Go

John 14:3

The importance of being ready to go was illustrated by the wildfires that recently devastated the high plains of Kansas. At times, the windblown fire was pushed by fifty- to sixty-miles-per-hour winds, and the fires traveled in excess of thirty miles per hour on the ground. If you were in the path of this monster and only one mile in front of it, that meant you had two minutes to evacuate and move out of the path of the flames.

It is easy to look back and say that those in the path of the fire should have been prepared. But what if the fire had been here instead of there? LaDonna and I were not prepared either. Two minutes! If we had faced this danger, we would have first contacted family members in our community to be sure they were getting out, doing so while driving to pick up my mom, grandkids, and daughter and son-in-law. That alone eats up our two minutes. No time to gather any valuables; no time to pack clothes; no time to do anything but leave.

God's Word tells us that Jesus Christ will take His church home to be with Him someday (John 14:3), and I firmly stand on God's Word that the time is close at hand. There will be no two-minute warning that time is about to expire. Instead, there has been a two-thousand-year warning, since Jesus walked this earth. There will be no time to make a quick phone call or grab something important. It's going to be instantaneous. I may not be ready for a disaster like a wildfire, but I am ready for Jesus to call His church to heaven. Are you ready?

March 19

Political Persuasion

Acts 1:1–5

If Jesus was living today as a human in the United States, would he be registered as a Republican or a Democrat? I know that is an absurd question, and I will admit that I honestly don't know, but it's something to consider. We know the godly values that Jesus lived, represented, and proclaimed during His thirty-three years of life, some two thousand years ago. I think that if Jesus was living among us today, those same values would be evident in absolutely everything in which He was involved, including being a registered voter!

Just as He was outspoken to the existing world then regarding the kingdom of God and proclaiming good news, I am convinced that Jesus would be doing those very same things if He was walking in human flesh among us today.

Jesus is not walking around in human flesh today, but you and I are His representation to a world that needs to hear good news. That's right! Registered Republicans and registered Democrats represent Jesus Christ. There are unattractive things in each platform, but as Christ's representatives, we are given the mandate to change the world, even turning the world upside down for the cause of Jesus Christ. If I say or do nothing, I automatically give my approval to the direction that is being driven by those with their hands on the steering wheel.

Jesus was a world-changing leader. Jesus is living today in the hearts and lives of human flesh. We are called to be world-changers and not onlookers.

Uncontrollable Excitement

1 Corinthians 2:6-10

Forty-nine years ago today (March 20, 1971 – March 20, 2020), my thoughts ran wild. I had not slept much during the night, due to my excitement for what the day would bring. This was the day I would marry my lovely and beautiful bride; the day I had dreamed of for what seemed to be a long time. Excitement had captivated my body, soul, and spirit. God was giving me the woman of my dreams, and I could barely contain all that I was experiencing. We had remained sexually pure until our vows were spoken, and I greatly anticipated what was waiting after the vows were spoken, after the reception, and after saying goodbye to those who had come to celebrate with us. I was not disappointed. The anticipation had been there for a long time, but we chose to wait until God's time, after we were married.

Often in life, we try to satisfy expectation too quickly and instead find dissatisfaction. God has a perfect plan for our lives, and often He allows excitement and expectation to become a significant part of what we experience. Don't hurry the experience! Allow it to unfold in God's perfect time. I assure you that God will bring satisfaction to the wait that is sometimes long, fulfilling the excitement and expectation with abundant satisfaction. After forty-six years, I am still filled with excitement and anticipation. Those early expectations were all surpassed by the reality of the experience—an experience realized in God's time and not rushed.

March 21

The Raging Battle

Isaiah 5:20

This world has two major forces waging battle for control. The battle (often referred to as a war) between good and evil has long existed. God's Word reveals that good will ultimately triumph over evil, but until that appointed time, the battle rages on. Warfare is not an idle amusement that is engaged in a frivolous manner. War is intentional and planned for with care. Several things are associated with war planning, including offensive and defensive maneuvers. Any living, breathing child of God can clearly see that the force of evil is on an offensive rampage. Viewed from a biblical perspective, it is a last-gasp effort to overturn the kingdom of God. That means that we, as Christians, must be in optimum defensive mode—not in defeat but in defending the faith. Sometimes the best defense is a great offense—an offensive lead by God Himself, with Jesus carrying the banner of victory. I am in the Lord's army. I have chosen the side of victory. Good wins. God wins! That is the ultimate headline.

March 22

Speak Out

Jeremiah 15:19 (NLT)

In Jeremiah 15:19, God was encouraging Jeremiah to be His spokesman for the people. Then God says this: "You are to influence others and not let them influence you" (NLT). I think most "solid" Christians have the not-being-influenced part down pretty well. From my observation, most of us need to work on the influencing-others part. Jesus said it this way: We must be salt and light.

What kind of influence does a little bit of salt have on meat? I enjoy smoking meat in my smoker—the smoke adds a lot of flavor. Before I place the meat in the smoker, I shake some salt all over the meat. By weight, the amount of salt is very small, but oh, the influence it has in allowing the meat to take in the smoke flavor and allowing the meat to be flavored by its own juices. Just a little salt makes a huge difference in the outcome.

A small nightlight gives enough light so that you won't stumble over an obstacle in the night. God's Word declares that we are to influence the world around us and not let it influence us. We must speak up and speak out words of influence in this world of wickedness.

Lord God Almighty, help me to influence my world for good and the things of God.

March 23

Bring It On

1 Chronicles 29:10–13

Signs of the spring season are all around. Fruit trees and other flowering trees are in full bloom and look beautiful. Some daffodils have bloomed, and other early spring flowers are getting close to showing their colors. For those of us living in the Plains of the United States, there is the wind. Spring is trying to push winter aside, but it doesn't go easily. We know by experience though, that winter will evolve to spring which in turn ushers in summer.

God's Word tells us that there will be signs indicating that the season of grace is nearing an end and that the taking away of the church of Jesus Christ and His Second Coming are at hand. We cannot be fooled into complacency and lack of interest, as we see these signs all around us. We must be diligent in our calling to share the gospel with every person. The enemy of our souls does not want to let go, much like winter, but the kingdom of God will prevail. I'm glad God has invited me to be a part of His kingdom. Join with me in proclaiming the message of His salvation.

March 24

Flee Wickedness

Psalm 37:23–27

The world around us continues to cascade down a steep slope of wickedness. Wickedness is so widely accepted that those involved even boast of their wickedness, laughing in the face of God and making it attractive to others to join in. God's Word says we are to flee wickedness. Fleeing is not stopping at the brink of wickedness and peering over the precipice at what is going on. Fleeing has the image of turning away and running for your life. Many times in the Word of God, God instructs people to flee. He told the people of Israel to flee Egypt, and we have the story of that flight in the Book of Exodus. God's instruction is to flee evil. I'm running for my life. Flee wickedness! Run for your life!

March 25

Intimacy—A Fact-of-Life Moment

Psalm 63:1–11

Intimacy is a seldom-discussed topic. Intimacy is a private matter that involves closeness, familiarity, and affection. To be biblically correct, sexual intimacy is between just two—male and female—married individuals. My question is this: Is intimacy important enough that we are teaching our children and grandchildren the value and importance of intimacy? Our world gets plenty of instruction on sex, plenty of direction on building relationships, and plenty of advice on how to succeed in life, but there is little instruction about the importance of intimacy.

Intimacy is vital to a marriage relationship, but it is also vital in our relationships with God. The Creator God of the universe desires an intimate relationship with each of us. The closeness and familiarity that are a part of intimacy leads us into knowing God more today than we did yesterday. It uses the alone time to bask in God's presence, just as we use the alone time in our marriage to strengthen that marriage. There is no set pattern or cookie-cutter method obtaining of intimacy. Intimacy is a learned art that is built and strengthened each time we participate. Just as a husband and wife long for those moments of intimacy, so God longs for intimacy with us. Let's enjoy intimacy with God and teach others the importance of intimacy—both physical and spiritual—as well.

March 26

Gods Mercy Is Brand New Today

Lamentations 3:21-26

Newness and freshness simply can't be replaced. There is nothing like the smell of a new car, the look of something that is fresh and new, or something that has been remodeled. Freshness and newness leave lasting impressions and fond memories in our lives. God's mercies are new every morning. Fresh and new, His mercies are like a breath of fresh air after a rain, a revitalization of the presence of a holy God that He provides to each of us every morning.

Let me encourage you to not live life by just remembering or living in God's mercies of yesterday or yesteryear. Live life immersed in the brand-new mercies God provides to you for this day and each day of life.

March 27

Control the Invasion

1 John 1:7–10

I spent some time earlier this week with the manager of a location of one of my distributors. We were going to look at a field of alfalfa several miles away. We drove past many acres of pastureland, and he would point out various invasive weed species that needed to be controlled in the next few weeks before they produced seed.

There are several options to control these invasive pests, but some application of control must be applied if any reduction of the pests is to be seen. His job as manager and the job of his sales personnel is to point out the problem to customers and give solid advice as to how to control the problem. There is some expense to controlling these invasive weeds, but the problem will become much larger and overtake usable pasture ground if not addressed now.

God spends considerable time in showing us, through His Word and through the revelation of His Holy Spirit, that there are invasive things—sins—that encroach upon our lives and that we must intentionally focus on removing them. Sometimes there is expense and even pain in doing so, but it must be done to keep the soil of our lives productive for the kingdom of God.

Lord God Almighty, show me the encroachment of the invasive sin in my life, and give me guidance in how to remove it. Help me to be willing to go to the expense and do what is needed to remove it from my life. Amen.

Now, has anyone seen the garden hoe?

March 28

Who We Secretly Are

Philippians 4:8

The innermost part of individuals is an important component of who they really are. What we secretly think and dwell upon has a dynamic impact on our lives and what others see and perceive in us daily. Each moment of each day, we choose what we want our minds to dwell upon. The apostle Paul gives this admonishment in Philippians 4:8 (AKJV):

> Finally, brethren, whatsoever things are true, whatsoever things are honest, whatsoever things are just, whatsoever things are pure, whatsoever things are lovely, whatsoever things are of good report, if there be any virtue, and if there be any praise, think on these things.

I have found that if you fill your life with this kind of thinking, there is no room for negative or evil thoughts. Think of the goodness of God today.

March 29

Budding Out

Isaiah 55:10

Trees are beginning to bud and leaf out in our area as our weather moderates into springtime. In our part of the world, we have many deciduous trees, meaning they lose their leaves in the winter and, though still alive, they look bare and dead. But during this dormant season, the roots have been aggressively growing and seeking out nutrients to start a new season and flourish in greater splendor than last year. I believe that the church of the living God has been in a dormant season for a time, but now that season is over, and the buds are beginning to show and burst forth in splendor. It is time for the church to come out of its dormant stage and flourish as God has intended it to—with all the power, gifts, and exploits that God has given to the church. It's a new season. Let's let God be God.

March 30

Amazed

Habakkuk 1:5 (NLT)

There is a line from a favorite song that is flowing through my mind today: "Prepare to be amazed." It is no coincidence that my Bible reading today contains this verse: "Look around at the nations; Look and be amazed. For I am doing something you wouldn't believe even if someone told you about it" (Habakkuk 1:5 NLT). We hear the phrase, "God is up to something," used when we sense that God is stirring His people, circumstances, plans, and outcomes. I have a deeply settled sense of the Spirit of God in my spirit, just simply saying, "Prepare to be amazed." How does one prepare to be amazed? For me, it will be watching for an opportunity for God to do the miraculous—and expecting Him to do so. I am watching, expecting, and preparing to be amazed by my amazing God.

March 31

Human Understanding

Isaiah 55:8–

When Jesus lived as a human on earth, He spent considerable time giving the disciples information about His impending brutal death and, ultimately His resurrection. The disciples were every bit as human as we are. When you have God's Son, the Messiah, living among you and walking with you, performing miracle after miracle, you just can't grasp hold of the idea that physical brutality and death would ever enter the picture. But it did, and it didn't happen without warning, even right up to the night Jesus was betrayed and arrested.

Today, God's Word gives us considerable insight and warning about last days and Jesus's return. While Jesus lived here on earth, His disciples wanted Him to be the Messiah who was the King of kings and the Lord of lords—the ruler of all the earth. But it was not yet His time. That time was in the future—a time we are fast approaching, a time that is at hand. Let me encourage each of us to know what God's Word says about the day in which we live. We cannot know the day or the hour, but we can certainly know the season.

April 1

Looking toward the Eastern Sky

Matthew 24:23–27

On Monday evening, November 14, 2016, with sunset to the west and moonrise to the east, the heavens produced a phenomenon called a supermoon. The moon was in its closest proximity to the earth in the last sixty-nine years. The Bible speaks significantly about signs in the heavens occurring as we approach last days here on earth. We recently experienced the blood moons that occurred prior to the US elections getting underway. A supermoon will make the moon appear larger than most of us have ever experienced in our lifetimes. I think it's not only interesting but of important note that the supermoon of 1947 occurred just prior to Israel becoming a nation on May 14, 1948. I do not have any divine revelation about the November 14, 2016 supermoon's occurrence, but with world events where they are, it is important that we recognize that this sign too points to humanity's place in time as being in "last days."

The evening of November 14, 2016, my focus was on the eastern sky for two distinct reasons: I desired to observe this supermoon, but most of all, I was and still am anticipating Jesus's return to this earth to take His children home. That event will far surpass any supermoon or blood moon in history. I'm looking up, and I'm looking eastward.

April 2

I Find No Fault

Luke 23:1–7

How easy it is to find fault in just about anything. A waiter brings table service to a group seated in a café, and the first request from someone in the group is to substitute the silverware with plastic utensils because the silverware was not clean enough. As the mealtime goes on, the faultfinder says the meal ordered was not prepared right, and the meat is not the right temperature. This person peppers the entire evening with finding fault, making the rest of the group uncomfortable.

Finding fault starts a cascade of tearing down relationships, friendships, and acquaintances. The trial of Jesus gives a good example of not identifying fault, when Pilate says, "I find no fault in Him." As Christians, God's Word clearly directs us to "build one another up in this most Holy Faith." Faults? Yes, I have plenty of them, but I'm glad that Jesus was willing to overlook my faults and saw my need to be built up and not torn down.

Let's take time to deliberately choose to flee finding fault and choose instead to build one another up. That's what Jesus would have us do. If you must find fault, find fault with the devil. There is plenty to find there, and you can satisfy your fault-finding need by doing so.

April 3

Out of the Mire

Psalm 40:1–3

We all face discouragement in our lives—times when things go wrong, or the momentum has disappeared, or the future has lost its attraction. After we have wallowed in self-pity, it's time to look to Jesus and let Him pull us out of the mire of discouragement. The Lord Jesus Christ is an encourager. He always calls us to greater things, testing us so that our mettle is pure. He lifts us up out of discouragement and sets us on a solid foundation of mercy and grace. For those who are discouraged this day, I offer this: You can continue to look at the things that have brought discouragement, or you can look to what God desires to bring into your life, focus on that, and be lifted out of your discouragement.

If you are discouraged today, God is not the source of that discouragement. God is the source of encouragement. May you be set lose from your chains of discouragement as you allow Jesus to take your hand and provide encouragement in your life this very moment.

April 4

I Really Didn't Want to Do That

Romans 7:15

As children of God, we know there are things God expects of us, and there are things God expects us not to be involved in. Sinful human nature struggles with being obedient to God's commands. Even the apostle Paul struggled with this, saying that his flesh wanted to do the things he knew he shouldn't do, and he didn't want to do the things that he knew he should do. But Paul, setting an example for each of us who follow Jesus, disciplined himself to be obedient into God. Discipline is a powerful influencer of how we conduct our lives—living for God or living in the flesh.

By the way, our lives are living testimonies to the discipline—or lack thereof—in our lives. Live a godly, disciplined life.

April 5

A Wise Choice

Matthew 19:16–22

Opposing viewpoints are an opportunity to carefully consider a differing view of subject matter. Often, insight is revealed that we otherwise would not see, and we can use this insight to strengthen a position. Jesus was talking to a rich young ruler about giving up all his possessions to be a part of the kingdom of God. We get insight to the young ruler's heart, as he goes away sad that he would have to give up so much.

Two viewpoints: one attracting the presence of God and enjoying the things that God would bring into his life; one looking at what he possessed and trusting that those possessions would remain. Having chosen to retain what he had, the rich young ruler went away sad. Don't let your viewpoint of what you possess today darken the potential to what God offers in serving Him. His way does not sadden us.

April 6

A Long and Fruitful Life

Jeremiah 17:7–8

I love the blooms of spring. The fruit trees, crab apple and ornamental pear, redbuds, and plum thickets all join in welcoming spring to our area. Also, the early flowers like tulips, daffodils, and many more add to this beauty. But shortly, the blooms pale and fall off, and the plants quickly become just a part of a not-so-significant landscape. I enjoy plants and trees that are long-blooming and add color all season long. These long-blooming plants remind me of the stability that God desires of me in life. These season-long blooming plants and trees endure storms, cold, heat, and drought but continue to produce colorful blossoms, despite the weather.

Lord God Almighty, I want to be like those plants and trees that are in bloom, no matter what the weather does. I desire that my life be attractive to others, no matter what I might face or go through. Jesus, I just want to be like you.

April 7

Who Is in Control?

2 Timothy 1:7

My choice to not consume alcohol or to even try life-controlling items, like tobacco and drugs, is a personal conviction supported by my faith. In my growing-up years, that choice made me a goody-goody. I am thankful to God that He placed in my life an intense desire to follow through with those convictions, even to this day. Did this separate me from my school friends? Yes, to some degree, but I still was friends with those who did indulge. I have friends today who are held in these vices, and as I look at my role as friend, I see myself as being an example of one who can live a fulfilled life without those vices. The world cannot conceive of giving control of one's entire life to God Almighty, in order to be in control of one's life.

If you have life-controlling things that affect your life today, giving those things—along with your entire life—to God is the only way you can be in control of your life. Jesus Christ is the way, the truth, and the life. Do life-controlling things have you locked in a vice? Give it wholly to God, and get back the control of your life.

April 8

A Rare Coin

Luke 15:8–10

Rarity of something of value increases its value. For instance, if you offered a 1944 steel wheat penny was worth one cent in 1944. If you used it as payment today for a Coke at a convenience store, it would still only be worth one cent. But because of its rarity, in the hands of a collector of rare coins, it is worth approximately $110,334. Our world is full of common and ordinary folks. I believe God's Word directs each of us who follows Christ to be that rare individual whose life lived for God makes him or her a highly valued individual. Of the trillions of pennies produced over the years, only a few are considered rare and worth more than one cent.

Lord God, make me to be like you—a valued, highly sought-after follower of Jesus Christ.

April 9

You Are of More Value than Many Sparrows

Luke 12:6–7

What's it worth? In part, it depends on who is valuing it. Consider a soul that has lost all hope, is homeless, hungry, and in the depths of despair. God gave His Son as a ransom to bring that soul back. A truckload of gold? God is using that as pavement in heaven. I love it when God takes something in which I can't see any value and makes it valuable. Sometimes the value is found in others, and sometimes the value is found in me. Let the God of all creation make something of value out of the worthlessness of what surrounds us today. He is able—more than able. You go, God.

April 10

That Fork in the Road

Proverbs 3:6

An often-used quote says, "When you come to a fork in the road, take it." We laugh at the simple concept, but it's true. Life continues down a pathway from birth until the end of our lives. This walk of life contains many forks in the road. If I sit at the intersection, pondering my direction, I don't get anywhere. I am not advocating irrational decisions, but if you have been sitting at the fork in the road for some time, then I have this from God's Word. If we have given our lives to God to serve Him and are obedient to His commands, His promise is that He will direct our paths, even placing the forks in the road at strategic places. If I select the wrong path, I have trust in God that He will close windows and doors that cannot be opened. If I have selected the right path and come to closed windows and doors, then I also trust God to open them—miraculously, if needed. Just sitting at the fork in the road doesn't get me anywhere.

April 11

What Happened between Jesus's Death and His Resurrection?

Revelation 1:18

Friday has ended with hours of unusual, black darkness. A man named Joseph has asked to take Jesus's body down from the cross and take it to a new, unused tomb. Because of the Sabbath starting at sundown on Friday, there was no time for a proper burial, only time to wrap Jesus's body in a white linen cloth and lay a smaller covering over His face and head. Proper burial for Jesus would have to wait until Sunday morning. Even though the curse of the Law had been broken on that Friday afternoon, Jewish law still had its grip on the culture, and the Sabbath was to be honored as before.

While the disciples scattered and the women closest to Jesus spent their Sabbath preparing to give Jesus a proper burial, Jesus was busy with something that needed to be done. The Bible does not say that Jesus went to heaven to be with His Father after His death or prior to His resurrection. God's Word says that Jesus spent time in hell, obtaining the keys to death, hell, and the grave from the fallen angel, Lucifer—the devil, Satan. For a while, the presence of the eternal, holy Son of God was in the very place where eternal punishment resides.

We often think about what it will be like to be in the presence of Jesus in heaven. Today, I wonder what it was like to have Jesus visit hell. I can only imagine because there are no written records, but I believe that when Jesus spoke, hell itself was shaken, and everyone there was silent, even in their agony of eternal damnation and torment.

God's Word says that Jesus wrestled the keys of death, hell, and the grave from Satan. I suspect that it was quite a wrestling match, and once again, the devil lost. The devil may be saying to you that he is winning the battle, but Satan is a liar. Because of what Jesus did on that Easter weekend in AD 33, he continues to be a loser. Jesus has obtained and won the victory.

Today, Jesus is shaking the keys of death, hell, and the grave as He holds them in His hand for all to see. That borrowed tomb, that temporary grave, will not retain Jesus. Sunday is only moments away.

April 12

He's Alive!

Matthew 26–28

The hours of the Sabbath had dragged by at a crawl. There was so much to contemplate, so much to process of the events that had taken place in the last week. Only one week ago, the people of Jerusalem had welcomed Jesus as a royal visitor. Jesus and His disciples would celebrate the Passover, and Jesus would give to them two very important commandments. Yet very quickly, one of Jesus's disciples would betray Him, the Son of God, and hand Him over to the temple authorities. The disciples would scatter like lost sheep, a mock trial would be held, and Jesus would be beaten and crucified. At the very moment of His physical death, the curtain in the temple that separated the presence of God from the world would be ripped apart, confirming a change in dispensations.

Humanity could now go boldly before almighty God Himself through Jesus Christ. Yet Jesus's body was cold and lying in a tomb, waiting for a proper burial. The Messiah, the promised leader of Israel, God's appointed one, was now dead, and all hope had been crushed. All the possibilities, all the dreams, all the hope of the world was now lying in a borrowed tomb.

But then, Sunday morning dawned.

It must have been a sleepless night for Mary as she planned just how she would prepare Jesus's body for a proper burial. We don't know for sure, but quite possibly she would have planned to wash the blood from Jesus's body and gently place as much of the ripped flesh back near where it belonged. She would then place burial spices around His body and gently wrap it for proper burial, all the while weeping.

As she rushed to the place where Jesus lay, she pondered who, at this very early hour, she could get to help move the heavy stone away from the opening of the tomb. Very quickly, she discovered that the stone had already been moved, and as she looked inside, she discovered that the tomb was empty. Her only thought was that someone had moved Jesus's body or had stolen it. She saw a man nearby and, assuming he was the caretaker, simply asked where they had taken the body of Jesus.

And then realization struck her. This was Jesus. Standing right there before her was the risen Savior. The Messiah. God's holy Son. Death had been defeated, and Jesus was alive.

April 13

Heaven's Dew

Deuteronomy 32:1–4

It was a lovely evening yesterday, and with the recent rains, the lawns have really grown fast and are lush. This is not a normal thing for our part of the world for late summer. I decided to mow after supper. It was perfect conditions when I started, but by the time I finished, the dew had come on, and it was just as if it had rained, though the sky was clear. We often think about God raining down blessings upon us, and that is wonderful when that happens. The dew that formed on my grass was a result of past rainfall and the right conditions. Those conditions were no wind, the right temperature, and a place for the dew to form.

My life in Jesus can be compared to this. I have had the blessing of God rained upon my life. But at times, it's important to recognize the dew that forms is a result of past rains and the right conditions. If God's blessings are not falling on your life like rain at this time, let me encourage you to set the right conditions—quiet your heart, calm your physical activity, and let the dew of past rains well up in your life. A heavy dew revitalizes, hydrates, and nourishes. Let the dew of God's blessings well up in your life today.

April 14

Quakes and Groanings

Romans 8:18–25

Our part of the world is shaking this morning with a 5.6 earthquake centered in Oklahoma; it was felt from Houston to Nebraska. We do not have mountains that break apart and fall into the valleys, nor do we have great canyons that cave in and stop rivers. We shake the ground and buildings and cause every dog to bark. We are not necessarily in an earthquake-prone area, but that didn't stop it from happening. God's Word declares that when sin is running rampant among the earth's inhabitants that the earth "groans."

The earth has been doing a lot of groaning lately. From the understanding of God's Word, we know that these types of events are related to the last days before end-time events. I believe that God's Word bears out the idea that these events will become more numerous and more powerful as we approach the day of Jesus's return to earth. I want to be ready for that day. I want to be ready for His return. I desire to leave this shaky ol' world and dwell in my mansion in heaven.

By the way, if you're shook up about the quake, the Bible also talks about hailstones that weigh seventy pounds. God will get man's attention. I desire to serve God today. He already has my attention.

April 15

A Trembling World

Ezekiel 38:17–23

Ezekiel, the Old Testament prophet, gives us a glimpse of what awaits a godless world that arrays itself against God's holy nation of Israel. In Ezekiel 38, the prophet writes that all living things will quake in terror at God's presence. Mountains will be thrown down, cliffs will crumble, and walls will fall to the ground. There is punishment of disease and bloodshed. In addition, there will be torrential rains, hailstones, fire, and burning sulfur. The prophet Haggai speaks about a great shaking that will take place. God will get man's attention one way or another. For me, God already has my attention, and I can see these things falling into place as nations and people begin to array themselves against Israel.

Don't wait until God draws the nations of the world, with a hook in their mouths, to come against Israel and then be slaughtered by God. There will be enough dead fighters that it will take seven months to bury the corpses. Let God have your attention now. Serving God during these times of intense godly judgment will be our only hope of survival.

Lord God Almighty, I give you my life and my attention today.

April 16

Seek Higher Ground

Habakkuk 3:18–19

Our area has been pounded with heavy rainfall. Some areas received four to twelve inches in just a few hours, and this caused major flooding in streams and rivers. There are reportedly missing individuals who drove onto flooded roadbeds during the night. Flooded roadbeds in our part of the world is uncommon, especially during late summer, and totally unexpected.

Our walks of faith sometimes meet with unexpected torrential happenings, catching us completely by surprise. A phrase has been repeated many times by weather media about our high rainfall event. "Turn around; don't drown." That can also apply to our spiritual lives. Sometimes it's important to just stop, turn around, and return to higher ground until the sun comes up or the flood recedes and reveals the roadway. Then we can see more clearly. Higher ground is a place of safety.

April 17

Come Before God with Boldness

Hebrews 4:16

If God has my attention—and He does—then how am I to respond to the almighty Creator? I could cower in great fear; that's how I view how many in the last days will react when God finally has their full attention. But cowering before the one who sent His Son to die for my sins isn't my idea of a proper relationship with the living God.

As Christians, we are taught to come boldly into God's throne room. That's a stark contrast to cowering before God. My relationship with my God gives me access to a holy God who has my best interest in mind. Yes, God has my attention, but I am not cowering in His presence. I am coming boldly before Him today and every day, through Jesus Christ, the Son. God's Word declares that no one comes to the Father except through Jesus, His Son. God has my attention, and I know Jesus as my Savior. I can come boldly into God's presence today.

April 18

Holiness Is a Requirement

Hebrews 12:14

One description of the individual who walks with God is that of holiness. We often talk about relationship, blessing, favor, goodness, and many other points of our walk with God, but little is said about holiness. God's Word says that without holiness, no one will see God. If I understand God's Word correctly, the central figure in heaven will be God on His throne, and all who are there will worship before He who sits on the throne. I believe that those who worship there will clearly see God. That makes holiness a requirement in my life to get to heaven and see God our Father. God's Word declares that my human holiness is likened to filthy rags, suitable only for throwing away. How, then, can I be holy before my God? Holiness can't be conveyed upon me by birth, national status, denomination membership, or even baptism. The only way that the holiness that God requires of me can be achieved is through Jesus Christ's redemption of my life by His sacrificing His life and covering me in His grace. Does that make me free to live an unholy life? Absolutely not. His sanctification of my life requires that I walk in holiness before God and His Son, Jesus, and before men. I must remember every moment of every day that without holiness, I won't see God. It's my desire to see God.

April 19

Focus and Attention Bring Wonderful Surprises

1 Samuel 3:1–11

Focused and attentive—sounds like an elementary classroom directive. But does that ever become obsolete? Probably not. I do lots of driving, and that statement applies. My job requires focus and attention. My marriage will survive only if I am focused and attentive. Lots of things call for my focus and attention as I go through life, but Jesus and what He did for me—and who He is to me today—demands that I willingly focus my attention on Him. I don't just do that because of obligation. I do it because of the surprise element that is God. If I am not focused and attentive, I may otherwise miss the constant, small, but still impactful surprises that God sends my way. And what I've found is that surprises from God always have a way of bringing God's best to my life. Surprises are God's way of rewarding our focus and attention. Don't be surprised if God surprises you today.

April 20

Grow Where You Are Planted

1 Corinthians 7:20–24

There is a place in New Mexico known for their green chilies. Known as Hatch chilies, these spicy peppers make their way into stores across the nation and are processed locally for distribution, even when out of season. What makes these peppers special is the soil and environment in which they are grown. Hatch, New Mexico, and the surrounding area is just the right place to grow these wonderful chili peppers. I have occasionally wondered why God "planted" me where I am and have come to these conclusions:

1. Sovereign God has a perfect plan for my life.
2. He knew that this environment would be just right for producing the best crop from my life. (Sometimes it's a harsh environment, but it produces great results.)_
3. He knew the wonderful care I could receive and from which I'd benefit by being placed here.

Grow where you are planted. God is a master gardener.

April 21

When Crisis Strikes

Matthew 11:28–30

A crisis will nearly always move us toward God. Whether personal, family, regional, national, or worldwide, a crisis always alters our direction in life and allows us to focus on God more than in the past. Does a crisis indicate that I am not a Christian or that I am outside His will in my life? Certainly, it can, but that's not necessarily so. I have been blessed to serve God all my life, and there have been crises in my life. Even in a strong relationship with God, the crisis would always move me closer to God.

Are you in the middle of a crisis? Let this situation move you closer to God from where you are today. If you do not know that Jesus Christ is your personal Savior, you can move from not knowing to assurance by simply asking Jesus into your heart and life and giving yourself completely into His love and care. You may need Jesus to wrap His loving arms around you and hold you tight. You need to let all the emotion that wells up within you pour out in sobs as He holds you tightly.

This I know: Jesus is touched by our feelings and emotions as we weep in His arms. Our deep emotions move God to action on our behalf. Don't allow a crisis to push you away from God. Let your crisis drive you into the arms of Jesus.

April 22

Peace of Mind

Numbers 6:22–26

Having peace of mind is a wonderful way to live. There is benefit in knowing that I can trust God. There are times when I feel like a young child who is being held up high in his father's arms at the edge of the Grand Canyon and dangling out over the edge. That child has no place to go but to trust in the one who is holding him.

As an adult I can choose to allow peace of mind to rule in my life, or I can worry, stew, or fret. Peace of mind is a much better option. There will be times when I have to trust God with my life as He holds me in a precarious situation, but I know who holds me. I know in whom I have believed, and I am persuaded that He is able to hold me securely in His arms. I have peace of mind.

April 23

I Need a Lamp

Psalm 119:105

My work requires that I travel overnight quite often. This means that I stay in a different hotel room every night I'm on the road. Most of the time, I will have one or two nature calls during the night. In a strange room, I can do one of two things: I can grope around in the dark and try to find my way, stumbling over the desk chair and coffee table and bumping into the wall; or I can switch on the bedside lamp and see clearly how to avoid all the obstacles.

Stubbornness will lead to stubbed toes and even a fall. It would be a quite simple act to turn on the lamp. Sometimes in our walk with God, we get stubborn and don't turn on the light. The psalmist expresses it this way in Psalm 119:105—"Thy word is a lamp unto my feet, and a light unto my path."

Friends, turn on the light of God's Word. It will keep you from stumbling and falling.

April 24

Do I Need Help?

Psalm 46:1–11

Can I help you, sir? Seems like more and more folks are offering to help me today. Must be my mature look and surely not my look of being lost. Most of the time I reply with *no thanks* because I think I've got it handled. The reality is, I'm really saying, "No, let me dig myself into more frustration, work, and turmoil"—it's amazing. The clerk could have quickly shown me where the canned yellow peppers were on the shelf. I spent several minutes looking and discovered I had walked past them at least two times. I should have been slapped silly.

Many of us are the same with God. God offers to help us, and our response is often, "No thanks. I think I can do it on my own." I'm a slow learner. But I recognize that when God asks, He sees something that I'm not seeing. Taking His help sooner rather than later saves a lot of time, turmoil, and frustration. Yes, there are times when I deserve a slap, a knock on the ol' noggin, or a kick in the shin for not accepting help when offered. Hey, those folks would really help if I would just let them.

April 25

Help Is Sometimes Delayed

Daniel 10:1–14

To believe that I can overcome the powerful influence of the enemy of my soul on my own is a lie to myself and to others. When we are deceived to this way of thinking, we grossly underestimate the power of the enemy of our soul.

God's Word gives us a glimpse of the power of the enemy. We are told the story of the man of God who prayed that God would send help, but none arrived. The man of God prayed for days, but no help arrived. Finally, help did arrive in the form of an angel, and when the man asked about the delay, the angel's reply, I was sent right away but encountered the devil's warfare on my way to minister to you. If even the angels of God have this kind of difficulty dealing with the enemy of our souls, how much more vulnerable am I, as a mere human? I need God's help and protection from the enemy of my soul. I can't do it on my own.

April 26

My Identification

Mark 16:15–18

Identification is an important part of our culture today. I must have proper identification to drive a vehicle, buy a plane ticket, or purchase items with a credit card. I carry proof of my identify in a driver's license, passport, and other items. In Mark 16, Jesus gave some examples of how the church of Jesus Christ would be identified—and even more so as we approach last days. I believe that the reality of God's expectation of the church is that this identity must always be shown and not in a vault under lock and key.

When I travel internationally, I always carry my passport in way it can be readily shown. I don't leave it at home. The church must exhibit the signs and wonders of God during these last days. Preach the good news to everyone. Cast out demons in Jesus's name. Be filled with the Holy Spirit and speak in tongues. They will place their hands on the sick, and they will be healed. That must be our identity as the living church of God in these last days.

April 27

Direct Access to the Throne of God

Hebrews 4:14–16

Though I am far from perfect (you may be nodding your head), I stand faultless before Father God. That is just plain amazing. How can this be, as I acknowledge my own imperfections? It is only because of the blood of Jesus Christ that has been applied to my life that I can stand before almighty God, and He won't turn away. God's Word declares that I personally can come *boldly* into the throne room of God, with Jesus Christ at my side, who will intercede on my behalf. Since the death and resurrection of Jesus Christ, the Son of God, I do not have to go through another man or woman—someone I may feel is closer to God than I am. I can go directly to God myself at any moment, any hour, and any day. Gone is the requirement that I go before a human priest. I can go before the *high priest*, Jesus Christ. Human representatives of God sometimes fail, as they are less than perfect. Jesus is perfect, and He will never fail. Place your complete trust in Jesus, and come *boldly* into God's throne room today.

April 28

New Skills

Jerimiah 32:26–27

A skill, while not a requirement, is a welcome attribute when beginning, doing, and completing a project. There have been times when I have undertaken a project for which I was not skilled, but at the completion, I had developed some skill—perhaps not as an expert, but certainly I was capable of seeing myself doing it again in the future.

All of us have done something for the first time and for which we had no skill, but by doing, we developed a skill that gave us an advantage in completing the task in the future. There are times though when my skills are is not enough, and I need to bring in an expert. The expert has a more developed skill set and can bring the project to its intended completion.

Sometimes as a Christian, God has me do new things for which I have not yet developed skills. In doing what God directs me to do, I develop the skills I need.

I love learning new skills, both in life and in the work of the kingdom of God. Sometimes, though, I need to call in the expert. God Himself declares that there is nothing too hard for Him. Now that's a skill set that I am glad is available to me, even as I develop skills of my own. His wisdom is far greater than human understanding. His skill set is out of this world.

April 29

A Change in Dispensations

Luke 1–2; Acts 2

In 2016, I read a chronological Bible. The last three days centered on the birth of Jesus. Centuries before and many generations prior to this historical event, God the Father focused attention toward this part of His plan for humankind. So impactful was Jesus's birth that even our calendar today reflects it. Jesus's birth changed the dispensation of time from that of law to one of grace. As Jesus walked among humans, it was God with us. That had not happened since God walked with Adam and Eve in the garden prior to the fall.

Even though God has been omnipresent for all eternity, He had not walked among humans until Jesus, the Son of God, did so. Jesus's human life ended at age thirty-three. God walking among humans had ended. But God had more—and I *love* more of a good thing. God walking among humans was a good thing, and His followers wanted more. But Jesus was gone, now walking in heaven among the angels.

The story of God walking among humans would end there, except for this. Jesus said, "I must go, but I will send to you the Holy Spirit." On that first Pentecost Sunday following Jesus's resurrection, Jesus did just that. Believers were filled with the Holy Spirit. Now men and women walked with the power of God within them. Thousands were saved on that day of outpouring. Why? Because God was walking through humans, not just among them. That Holy Ghost power has never been withdrawn. As a Christian, I must be an individual filled with the Holy Spirit. God walks this earth through me and every Spirit-filled believer. Be filled with the Holy Spirit!

April 30

Not a Normal Church Service

Matthew 3:1–12

John the Baptist preached a message of repentance and water baptism. In Matthew 3, we find that a crowd of religious leaders had come to see what was going on. This activity was certainly not a part of the required temple worship routine, but many had responded to John's message and were repenting and being baptized in water. As the religious leaders looked on, here's what happened:

> But when he saw the Pharisees and Sadducees coming to watch him baptize, he denounced them "You brood of snakes," he exclaimed. "who warned you to flee the coming wrath? Prove by the way you live that you have repented of your sins and turned to God. Don't just say to each other, 'we're safe, for we are descendants of Abraham. That means nothing." (Matthew 3:7–9 NLT)

Being a descendent of a godly individual means nothing regarding our salvation. Belonging to a church denomination or organization means nothing. Only our salvation through the blood of Jesus Christ will have meaning when we stand before eternal God.

Water baptism is a public declaration of what God has done in our lives. John's words are as applicable today as they were on the day he spoke them. Prove by the way you live that you have repented and turned to God. God is simply saying to us today that we must prove the work of His salvation in the way that we live.

Jesus, I don't just want to say that I'm a Christian. I desire to *be* a Christian.

May 1

Weeds in Crops

Matthew 13:24–30

A good plant out of place is considered an unwanted weed. I live in the farm plains of the USA. A lot of farmers rotate their fields between soybeans and corn. When soybeans follow corn, there is always "volunteer" corn that grows up within the field of soybeans. Both plants are a desirable crop, but corn growing in a soybean field is undesirable and makes it a weed is out of place. There are various ways of removing the undesirable corn, from hand removal to herbicide control.

Sometimes personalities of human beings are similar to this. Sometimes a personality just doesn't fit in the "field." If that's true in your life, then perhaps a "transplant" is needed. Removing yourself from the field is a viable option. It's good to grow where you were planted, but sometimes you might find you are in the wrong field. God will give direction and solid advice. We only need to ask.

May 2

Be Filled with the Spirit

Ephesians 5:1–21

As our world rushes headlong into situations and world events that define biblical last days, it is becoming increasingly evident that Christians must be full of the power of God to stand in these times. Human power will fail miserably. Only by the power of God living in us and through us, as the living Spirit of God dwelling in our lives, will we be able to stand on the solid rock of Jesus Christ.

When you stand on the rock, you make a good target for the enemy of your soul, but when you stand on that rock full of the Holy Spirit, you have the power of God defending you. We are told in very explicit words in the scriptures that having done all to stand, we are to stand clothed in the armor of God. I am standing on the rock today, full of God's Spirit but desiring even more of God's Holy Spirit living through me.

Be filled with the Spirit. It's not a suggestion; it's a command!

May 3

You Can Do That

Philippians 4:12–13

I can't do that! As Christians, we have all responded at some time with those words to God's request for us to do something. God says we can. Our physical nature says we can't.

God's Word says I can do *all* things through Christ who strengthens me.

I am not here to tell you what God is telling you to do. God is fully capable of doing that Himself. I'm here to tell you that you *can* do it, no matter how hopeless or helpless you feel. Satan would have you stay defeated. God says you can do it through His power and His help. Yes, you can!

May 4

Press In and Touch God

Luke 8:43–48

Luke 8 contains the story of the woman who had the issue of blood for many years. When Jesus came to her community, she came to Him for healing but could only get close enough to touch the hem of Jesus's garment. In doing so, she obtained her healing. Jesus knew that healing virtue had gone from His body, and He simply asked, "Who deliberately touched me?"

The woman had made a concentrated and deliberate effort to get her healing from Jesus. Because she could only get close enough to touch His garment, she pressed in and took that opportunity. She did not wait for him to get to the edge of town, where the crowd might thin out. She pressed in, in the thick of the crowd, and got what she was after.

What do you desire from God that you are willing to press in to the crowd and touch Jesus to receive it? You don't need to wait until Jesus is at the edge of town and the crowd has thinned. Don't make it a half-hearted effort. Deliberately press in, and obtain what you desire from God.

May 5

God Does Not Forget

Proverbs 3:1

I forgot. It's a simple and common mistake that we all make from time to time. We promise or commit to something and then forget. It's a human tendency that plagues the human species. The Word of God contains thousands of promises—some 5,467, if you are counting—and God does not forget one of them. He never forgets His faithfulness and mercy, though we sometimes forget or perhaps ignore it.

God loves you, and He cares about you completely. Don't forget!

May 6

A Hungry Crowd

Matthew 14:13–21

As humans, we tend to look at circumstances from a mostly practical viewpoint. When Jesus fed the five thousand men, plus women and children, He asked where they could buy food enough to feed the crowd. I'm just guessing, but I don't think there were enough convenience stores, grocery stores, or cafés to even begin supplying the amount of food it would take to feed this multitude. Then one of the disciples looked at the situation from a practical viewpoint and said that even if there was a place to buy the food, they would have to work many months to be able to purchase everything needed.

Jesus also viewed the circumstance from a practical viewpoint. He saw a crowd that had grown physically hungry as they had listened to His teaching. It was a logical question to ask—*Where can we buy enough food to feed these hungry people?* Jesus knew what He was about to do but wanted to test the disciples as to where their faith was. The practicality of the matter was that people were hungry and needed food at that time. There was no place close enough to buy that much food, and there was not enough money to buy whatever food was available. The disciples looked at the situation from a practical point of view and saw the hungry but did not see any practical way of dealing with it.

Jesus saw the immediate need but also saw the need for a practical answer from a perspective of the miraculous. The crowd was hungry at that moment. Waiting was not an option. Feeding them at their point of need was practical from all viewpoints, but only the miraculous would handle the immediate need.

If you are viewing a need from your human practicality, and the answer is impossible or nearly so, I am here to tell you that Jesus is also looking at your circumstance from a practical viewpoint—only His viewpoint is not clouded with impossibility. Jesus's viewpoint is wrapped in miracles. Let the impossible become reality through Jesus.

May 7

We Have All Sinned

Romans 3:21–25

As our world of politics continues the game of guilt and blame, I want to remind us that God's Word declares that we are all guilty of wrongdoing, and we are stand at a place of blame before others and before God. Only when Jesus offered forgiveness, and I repented did my guilt and blame before Him disappear. The world might remember all of it, but God has forgotten all of it, if I have confessed it before Him.

We cannot look on others and compare who had less sin. We must point others in a direction toward God and the forgiveness He offers through Jesus Christ. Not one of us can stand before our world without someone finding blame or guilt in us. But we can stand and say that eternal God has forgiven us, and we stand in His presence as His children. We must point those who desire to serve in elected government toward the one who can forgive completely and turn a life around, and they should begin serving God.

May 8

God's Favor

Isaiah 58:11, Psalm 5:12

God's favor has rested on the United States for over 240 years. I was fortunate to have been born here and to live my life under this favor. This favor and life we have is quite attractive to many who were not fortunate to be born here, as indicated by the large number of people desiring to come to this country, both legally and illegally. For many, there is desperation in their actions, and for some, there are evil motives for coming here.

Early in the history of our nation, the attraction was religious freedom and open worship of God. Now, the attraction seems to be financial opportunity, drugs, or other evil activity that draws people. Unfortunately, the attractions are not the things of God. The church of the living God must exist and be full of the living, moving Holy Spirit. When that happens, there will be an abundance of God things and an attraction that cannot be ignored or overlooked. When there is that type of attraction, there will be tremendous opportunity for changed lives for eternity.

Living God, I desire that my church be full of Your living presence and have the power of Your Holy Spirit, moving in such a way that there will be an overwhelming attraction to those who need salvation, healing, restoration, and miracles in their lives.

I have experienced God's favor, but there is so much more to experience—and I want it all.

Unwanted Weeds

Matthew 13:24-30

A dorm building is under construction at the Woodston campgrounds. The basement walls were built several months ago, and then the work stopped until funds could be raised to continue building. This week, they're preparing for the concrete basement floor to be poured. During the period since construction stopped, many large weeds have grown up in the floor area and will now have to be removed before we can move forward. This will require digging up each plant by the root and physically removing it from the site.

If we are not careful to maintain our spiritual growth with Jesus Christ, unwanted things probably will crop up in our lives.

If we'd taken care of it earlier, we could have easily pulled the weeds up without the need of a spade. Now they have a very extensive root system, and the removal process is a lot more intense.

If we have allowed something undesirable to take root and haven't removed it right away, the removal later will require a lot more effort and will perhaps even be painful. Be careful in your spiritual life to not let undesired things take root in your life. If you discover that there is something undesirable there, remove it right away. Don't let it grow to maturity and then try to remove it.

Mothers

Proverbs 4:3; 6:20

I have been blessed to have two moms in my life. One is my Mother, Wanda, whom God has allowed to be part of my entire life, and one is my wife's mother, Gladys, whom we also called Mom. Gladys was Mom to me for some two-thirds of my life. Both women were wonderful, beautiful, godly women who had a profound impact on their families.

In her later years, LaDonna's mother had beautiful white hair. One luxury that she indulged in was going to the beauty shop every Saturday to get her hair done. She always looked forward to these outings, and she always came home with a glow (could it have been a halo?) surrounding her.

LaDonna's father died when she was ten, and her mom was left to raise the four youngest girls and a son out of their ten children. Mom had to learn to drive, work to support a family, and move at least twice, while keeping her family together.

Attending church was a normal family function, and it was in church that I met LaDonna. (Thank God for faithful people who attend church. You just might meet your future spouse there.)

I came to discover that our moms have a different outlook on life. It was my mom who taught me to put on clean underwear each day, "Just in case you are in an accident." So far, the accidents I have been in have not required me to strip down to my underwear, but I am prepared. (My family is rolling their eyes.) It was my mom's responsibility to get four boys ready for church and make sure we were in the car, ready to make the twenty-minute drive to be at the church fifteen minutes early. In those days, the fellowship time occurred before the service started and then continued after the service was over.

The godly influence that these two moms had on their families will not be fully known until we get to heaven. The sometimes mundane, tedious task of being a mom starts when that first baby is born and continues for the rest of her life. Our moms have been the best.

Mom, LaDonna and I have been blessed because of your faithfulness in serving God, no matter what comes your way or how life treats you.

Thank you, God, for the privilege of having two wonderful moms.

Godly mothers—we are blessed.

May 11

The Beginning

John 1:1

Eight-Day Scripture Challenge

Day one—John 1:1 (New Living Translation)

> Prologue: Christ, the Eternal Word
> In the beginning the Word already existed.
> The Word was with God, and the Word was God.

I do not usually do Facebook challenges, but I have a granddaughter who wants me to accept this challenge, and so I will. These seventeen words found in John 1:1 fully describe the eternal God in the person of Jesus Christ. For human understanding, there must be a beginning. At that beginning place, Jesus, the Son of the Triune God, had always existed. He forever was, He is with Father God today, and He will exist for eternity future. As my finite mind wraps itself around the infinite existence of God, I am humbled in the presence of the Holy God as Father, Son, and Holy Spirit. They are awesome. And I know them.

May 12

A Quiet, Tender Moment

Deuteronomy 32:2

Eight-Day Scripture Challenge

Day two—Deuteronomy 32:2 (New Living Translation)

> Let my teaching fall on you like rain; let my speech settle like dew. Let my words fall like rain on tender grass, like gentle showers on young plants.

I have used this scripture twice in speaking to a younger generation in Peru, South America. I think it has application to what I post here every day. Our day is filled with words. Some are meaningful and some are not. Some bring hurt and pain; some bring healing. Some words give direction, while some just add to the confusion. Some words are gentle, but many are harsh. Our words are a vocal expression of who we really are. We are measured by the words we speak and how we speak them. The tone of our voices is a strong indicator of our deep emotions. The little preschool song says it best: "Be careful, little mouth, what you speak."

Father in heaven, the above scripture is my prayer.

Quiet on the Set

Psalm 46:10

Eight-Day Scripture Challenge

Day three—Psalm 46:10 (NLT)

> "Be still and know that I am God! I will be honored by every nation. I will be honored throughout the world."

As a young boy, I was admonished to "be still" countless times. This was long before attention deficit disorder was talked about. I was just a normal boy with lots of energy and a need to move about. "Be still," coming from the lips of my parents or a teacher in school, meant that I was too active, doing my own thing, and I needed to settle down and fully engage in what was happening in the classroom or at home.

Life is filled with doing things, some of which are needed, but as I observe the culture around me, some things we do are our "own things." God, our Father, God our Teacher, says to all of us, "Be still and know that I am God."

I often find myself with too much going on, and most of the time, it is because of doing my own thing. When I find myself overwhelmed, I need to settle down, get still, and know God and know that He can do the impossible—heal the sick, open blind eyes, change circumstances, and relieve the suffering. It's God speaking: "Be still."

This Is Really Good. Come On—Taste It

Psalm 34:8

Eight-Day Scripture Challenge

Day four—Psalm 34:8 (NLT)

> Taste and see that the Lord is good.
> Oh, the joys of those who take refuge in him!

I enjoy eating. One of my favorite foods is smoked baby back ribs. I have devoured these scrumptious, exquisite, delectable taste treats that have been smoked with various woods, including hickory (my favorite) mesquite, apple, cherry, oak, apricot—the list goes on. Each wood gives the smoked meat a distinct taste, and I enjoy them all.

Not only can you enjoy the taste of your favorite wood smoke, but you can apply your favorite barbecue sauce for added taste. I have found many different barbecue flavors, even root beer and Dr. Pepper, that can enhance the taste of already-tasty ribs.

The psalmist invites us to "Taste and see that the Lord is good." I have found that God's goodness does indeed taste great. There is a distinct and flavorful palatability when God is in my life. When something tastes good, we desire more than just a taste. We want to have our fill of what we have tasted.

God's Word proclaims this to those who taste the Lord: "Oh, the joys of those who take refuge in Him." If you are missing joy in your life, go back to the table of God and taste His goodness. Perhaps you have had a taste before but have stepped away from the table. I assure you there is an open place at God's table. Go back and have a seat. Grab a platter, and dig in.

May 15

A Need for Wisdom

James 1:5

Eight-Day Scripture Challenge

Day five—James 1:5 (NLT)

> If you need wisdom, ask our generous God, and he will give it to you. He will not rebuke you for asking.

It seems like it's always easy to ask God for "stuff," but I must ask myself if it's the *right* stuff. Sometimes God's Word is very clear on what we can ask God for. In the case of wisdom, this verse is very clear. If I need wisdom, I am to ask God. But that is *not the end* of the matter. God gives it—wisdom. Not the world's wisdom but His godly wisdom.

And I am not rebuked for asking. An intimate God wants to give me—and each of us—wonderful and awesome wisdom. And all I need to do is ask. Lord God Almighty, I ask for Your wisdom for every decision I face today, tomorrow, and throughout my life.

May 16

God Made Man

Genesis 2:7

Eight-Day Scripture Challenge

Day six—Genesis 2:7 (NLT)

> Then the Lord God formed the man from the dust of the ground. He breathed the breath of life into the man's nostrils, and the man became a living person.

There is something of a mystery about the breath of God. In this factual account of the creation of man, we find that God simply breathed into the nostrils of man, Adam, and man became a living person. In the factual account of Pentecost that occurred fifty days following Jesus's resurrection, we find that, once again, God "breathed," as evidenced by the sound of a mighty rushing wind. When God breathes, life happens, the spirit of the individual is set free, and the world around us is changed for the better. I want God to breathe into my life. I desire the life-changing, wind-sweeping, earth-shattering breath of God to sweep over me.

My Rock

2 Samuel 22:1–4

Eight-Day Scripture Challenge

Day seven—2 Samuel 22:3 (NLT)

> My God is my rock, in whom I find protection. He is my shield, the power that saves me, and my place of safety. He is my refuge, my savior, the one who saves me from violence.

Knowing in whom I trust is a powerful force in my life. Why can I stand firm when the world around me crumbles? Why can I have peace in the midst of a storm? Why can I stand still while the enemy of my soul shoots fiery arrows at me? Why can I trust that everything will be OK? It is because of the rock of my salvation, Jesus Christ. He is all that is described in this verse.

A Clear Choice
Joshua 24:14–15

Eight-Day Scripture Challenge

Day eight—Joshua 24:15 (NLT)

> But if you refuse to serve the Lord, then choose today whom you will serve. Would you prefer the gods your ancestors served beyond the Euphrates? Or will it be the gods of the Amorites in whose land you now live? But as for me and my family, we will serve the Lord.

Choosing to serve the Lord is a daily choice. Making sure your family is serving the Lord is a daily task, even when you have adult children and grandchildren who are entering adulthood. I don't sit down each day and spend twenty minutes deciding if I should serve the Lord. I decide the moment I wake up in this new day that I am going to serve the Lord and not follow the gods of this world. I then live that choice and try to add influence on my family to do the same. There is no better choice in this life than serving the Lord.

May 19

Repentance—A Vital Component of Salvation

2 Peter 3:8–10

I believe that God can and does forgive all sin, even the greatest of our sin. He does so willingly and out of a compassionate heart. To receive His forgiveness, all God asks is that we come to Him with repentance. How does one repent? First, God places within the soul of an individual a recognition of the sin that separates one from God. There are two responses possible when we come to that realization: (1) we can just ignore it, push it away, say no, and remain separated from God, or (2) we can let the realization move us to a place where we desire the close fellowship of God and desire to turn from the sin in repentance, asking for God's great forgiveness and forcibly moving our lives in the opposite direction from where sin was taking us.

Repentance is a willing desire that wells up within us to do what is necessary to eliminate the sin from our lives. Can I be forgiven without repenting? Yes, God can forgive without repentance, but the work of the Holy Spirit is to convict us of sin—sin that separates us from God. And that conviction leads us to repentance.

Our churches have great messages of forgiveness. A relationship with God goes beyond just my benefit of forgiveness. Repentance draws me closer to God in fellowship that is beneficial for both of us.

May 20

Four Days Late

John 11:1–44

Jesus's friend Lazarus had become sick, and his sisters, Mary and Martha, had sent for Jesus to come because they believed Jesus could heal their brother. Jesus received their request, then waited two days before going to his friend's hometown. During this time, Lazarus died.

Death has a finality. Gone is the ability to get well or to heal. Death ends the living life. Lazarus had been dead and buried for four days when Jesus arrived. He was met with these words from Lazarus's family: "If you had just been here, Lazarus would be well." Now it was too late. Death had cast its mark on Lazarus's life. All hope was gone.

At this point, Lazarus's body was decaying and stinking, further pronouncing the finality of death. But Jesus, four days late, was still there. The one who would Himself soon go to His own grave and rise victorious over death spoke life into Lazarus's lifeless and decaying body. Lazarus walked out of the grave, bound hand and foot in the grave clothes that had been placed on him.

Friends, when hope is gone and finality has set in, Jesus can come along and speak life into that hopeless situation. Let Jesus do that for you today. You may think that it's too late and a hopeless cause, but it is not when Jesus comes on the scene. Invite Jesus to come and to take care of your situation. Jesus is not powerless, even when He is four days late.

May 21

Working Perfectly

Hebrews 3:12–19

Occasionally, I get an email from my company, Help Desk, letting me know that some segment of our technology applications is not working properly. When I receive these notes, they have already brought in professionals to remedy the problem, even if it is at night or on the weekend. I appreciate the fact that they don't leave the situation pending until a better time. They take care of it now.

How many times in my own life has something gone wrong, and rather than fix it immediately, I put it off until a better time? And I usually would wind up paying for it in lost ability, lost time, or lost resources. It is always beneficial to take care of problems early on rather than later.

You may have (and I have as well) spiritual deficiencies that need fixing. It's easy to wait for a better time, but it's not the most beneficial response. As God shows us our need and sends us a "note," we would do well to take care of it now—today, while it is yet day.

By the way, the Help Desk just sent another note that the issue was resolved. We are functioning as we should.

May 22

A Second Language

Romans 8:26–27

I met a lady yesterday who is nearly one hundred years old. Her son said that she was bilingual. I caught on very quickly that he was talking about her being filled with the Holy Spirit, and her second language was a Holy Spirit language. That set me to thinking of my own life. Am I known as bilingual regarding the Holy Spirit language applied to my life? Many times, I know the specifics of how I should pray, but most of the time I don't know all there is to know about what I am praying for.

God's Word teaches us that the Holy Spirit, praying through our hearts and minds and spoken out of our tongues and lips in a language unknown to us, is God praying perfectly through us by the power of the Holy Spirit. I like perfection, and the things of God are perfect. Praying a perfect prayer about someone or a specific situation is much more desirable than my attempt to pray in my native language from my own viewpoint.

Is there someone you desire that God would intervene in their life and do the miraculous? Then if you are filled with the Holy Spirit, pray in your Spirit language. God as Holy Spirit will pray perfectly through you. If you feel inadequate in your prayer life, be filled with the Holy Spirit, as evidenced by speaking in a language you do not understand, but God understands because He gives it to you. Be filled with the Holy Spirit. Pray perfectly as the Holy Spirit prays through you. As a Christian, I want to be known as bilingual.

May 23

Review the Past—Look Ahead

Isaiah 26:3–4

In a couple of days, the account managers in my sales area will sit down together and analyze this past year and discuss plans for the coming year. Planning the future without looking back is not advisable in business, or in life, or in politics. In all three, it's important to look back and then make changes to improve the future. Our sales group will not go blindly uninformed into the next year because we choose to have this review time and carefully plan for the coming year.

As we go to the voting booth in future elections, let us be sure to review the past so that we can carefully plan the future. Make your vote count. And make it count for godly principles.

May 24

Watch

Mark 13:1–37

Jesus is speaking in Mark 13. At the end of the chapter, Jesus talks about His Second Coming to earth. In the last words of the chapter, Jesus says we must *watch*. Our world is full of things that entice us to watch. The political races, the world happenings, weather, even our family activities need to be watched.

I plan to watch the election returns the evening of the election. I plan to watch my grandchildren in their Christmas programs. But am I watching for the return of Jesus as He told me to? I'm watching and waiting. I'm anticipating as never before.

Lord God Almighty, don't allow me to get so caught up in watching these other things that I forget to watch for Your return. Even so, come, Lord Jesus. My focus is toward the eastern sky.

May 25

Charting a New Course

James 1:21–27

November 2016. Today our nation embarks on a new course. We are on this ship together and know that it will not always be easy sailing, but let's stay the course toward a better America. Let's focus on making America great again. We do that by making the Lord God Almighty our nation's Lord. When this nation makes the one living God our Lord, then we can also have His favor.

This nation has stood on the brink of disaster and has been pulled by the enticement of the enemy of our souls to go down a slippery slope of sin and degradation. Our nation has just managed to grasp hold of the last bit of stability that remains of godliness and morality. Let's not just hold on, but let's each of us do our part to put ourselves back in God's favor and right standing before God Almighty. We are not on a cruise ship. This is the ship of Zion. All aboard!

May 26

God Intervenes in the Affairs of Individuals

Psalm 77:10–15

One thing is certain: God was not surprised by the election results of November 2016, nor was he surprised by where the winning votes came from, and no, it wasn't from the "backward rural American population." The rural and farm communities of this nation voted in unprecedented numbers along with evangelicals and effectively put the brakes on, even if just for a little while, America doing a nose dive into a place of total unrighteousness and godlessness that would have most certainly demanded the quick judgment of God in this country that we love.

America now has an opportunity to pause for a moment and consider the path that we have been on—a path that has taken us deeper into sin and farther away from God and closer to God's final judgment. We have an opportunity to pray, in numbers of believers that are too great to count, that God will forgive this nation and restore us to greatness before Him and the world around us.

We have an opportunity to be the church that God desires us to be and to display the power of God working through us. Church of the living God, it is our time. It is our season. It is our responsibility. It is our destiny.

One Holy Spirit; Two Impacts

Acts 2:1–47

The impact on this world and its inhabitants immediately following the outpouring of the Holy Spirit on the day of Pentecost was twofold. Our attention focuses on the power and authority with which those filled with the Holy Spirit preached, taught, and performed miracles and saw the church membership increase in dramatic numbers in a short time. But there was another group that was not thrilled with what was happening—the religious leaders, the ones who had Jesus brutally killed to do away with God living among humankind. Their reaction to what was happening to the church was wondering how it would end. The church of the living God was looking to see how far it would expand.

Our world today is filled with people. Many are "religious" but are still waiting for the end of it. I declare to you today that there will never be an end to it until God Himself removes the church of the living God. As we approach what we know to be last days, let the power of God fill our lives to the point that we boldly proclaim Jesus Christ in every home, every situation, every circumstance, every place of worship, every office, every place of business, every government building, every school, and every college. Let us be so full of the living God that when we pray for people to be healed, they are immediately made whole. When we pray for a circumstance, it is changed powerfully by an intervening God. Don't sit idly by and wonder how it will end. Step in with the power of the living God and expect the church to expand in miraculous ways.

Do You Want to Be Made Well?

John 5:1-9

Committing your life to a full year of developing a new life in Jesus Christ and His power to change you completely is a huge step. It's a period of time that will transform your life. If you are dealing with life-controlling issues that have you bound and that you have tried to change, but you are locked into these habits, dependencies, and failures, let me recommend Teen Challenge*. One year of intense Bible Training and resolving life controlling habits seems to be an unacceptable time to be away from family and friends to devote yourself to change, but if you look at it from the perspective of a full, productive life and a lifetime of seventy years, it is only a 1.5 percent investment of your lifetime. Pretty small in the grand scheme of things It's a one-year commitment, but it's a year that will change your life for the good and will make a huge difference in who and what you depend upon.

You may have tried the other stuff, the other programs, the alternatives, and your own will to change, but it has all ended in failure. Do you want to change? Do you want to be made well and made whole? One year—your commitment to give your life to God and to give one year of your life to life change. One year with Teen Challenge, and you can say, "It is well with my soul, and it is well with my life.

*Teen Challenge is an adult and teen focused treatment program with facilities worldwide that centers on transformation not rehabilitation. Most Teen Challenge residential programs last 12-18 months under supervised instruction.

* (www//teenchallengeusa.org)

Sick and Afflicted

James 5:14–16

We are sick and afflicted. I don't mean that we are staying home with the flu or other ailment that keeps us in bed. I recently observed an altar call from the pastor of a church; he simply asked for those in attendance who needed healing in their bodies to stand to their feet. To look out over the congregation, you would know some there needed healing, but most appeared to be well. I was shocked when nearly every person in attendance stood up in response to the pastor's request. Nearly everyone in attendance in a large congregation had some ailment, disease, or medical, emotional, or physical issue going on in their bodies.

We are sick and afflicted. In a culture that has an abundance of medicine, medical procedures, and cures, we are sick and afflicted. As I consider who will be in the church service that I will attend this morning, I realize a great percentage currently are taking medication for an ailment or fighting physical disease or an emotional battle. We are sick and afflicted.

Lord God Almighty, as we see You responding to our prayers to heal our nation, may we also pray for each other for physical healing, miracles of healing to take place, and lives delivered from affliction. God, you are able to do exceedingly and abundantly far more than we can ask or even think.

My God delivers from affliction, completely and without reoccurrence. Almighty God, heal your people as we gather in houses of worship today.

If you need God's healing touch today, reach out to Him in faith, and be made whole.

May 30

Please Stand by for a Special Announcement

Matthew 24:15; Mark 13:14

Hold the phone; stop the presses; this special bulletin just in; amber alert. All these short statements are designed to capture our attention and stop our current activity so we pay attention to what will be said. There are two places in God's Word in the New Living Translation of the Bible where the following words are placed in parentheses: (Reader, pay attention). Found in Matthew 24:15 and Mark 13:14, both attention-grabbing statements refer to the signs pointing to "the sacrilegious object that causes desecration standing where it should not be." God's Word is full of messages and proclamations that are important to pay attention to, but when we see the words "Reader, pay attention," that has a special added emphasis.

Some good things are happening in our nation currently, and I am thankful for that, but my eyes must be fastened on what is happening with the nation of Israel and all that is taking place in the Middle East. Obvious signs of the times point toward the reality that the one who will be the Antichrist is now living on this earth. God's Word is very clear and of special, attention-grabbing importance. Reader, pay attention.

May 31

Return on Investment

Luke 6:36–38

I consider the "giving of thanks," in part, to be an investment. Too often, routine duties are performed without thanks. Meals prepared, clothes washed (and put away), house cleaned, bills paid, warm sheets on cold nights, cool sheets on summer nights—the list is endless.

For over forty-eight years, these routine chores have been completed in our home by my bride. Sometimes I do remember to say thanks. The chores get done whether I say thanks or not, but when I compliment her and say thank you, taking time to acknowledge the time, energy, and talent involved in doing these chores, I always get a positive return—a return on my investment.

At a time when monetary returns on financial investments are very weak, perhaps we should focus on investments of giving thanks. The return on investment is far greater than financial reward. Thank you, LaDonna, my wife, for being God's greatest gift—far more than I could ever have asked, dreamed, or hoped for. Thank you for being mine to hold and cherish and, most important, to love. That is more important than any financial reward that may come my way. Thank you for being the love of my life.

June 1

And the Two Shall Become One

Mark 10:6–12

"And the two shall become one." That statement found in God's Word is a statement both of mystery and of power. I direct my comments today to those who are married or are contemplating marriage in the future. LaDonna and I have been married for nearly forty-nine years. During that time, we have found each other's weaknesses and faults (I am ahead of her in number in both categories), things that could have easily pried us apart.

But we have chosen a different path—a path to confirm each other's strengths and to push each other to greater things, and in doing so, we have found the power and strength to become one in a bond that will not easily be broken. My challenge to those who are married, on this day and every day forward, is to concentrate not on weakness but on strengthening your relationship. Be thankful that you are not alone and that you have the strength of your life partner to bridge your weakness. Using your strength to build a bridge for your spouse's weakness only confirms that God's Word states that the two shall become one. Your soul's enemy and the enemy of your marriage would tear you apart and cause your marriage to fail, but God has a different plan. It's a plan of unity, a plan of wholeness and wellness. It's a perfect plan—a plan for the two to become one.

June 2

Freedom or Imprisonment

Ephesians 5:1

For all my life, Cuba has been under Communist control—a socialist state that has burdened Cubans with poverty and low esteem. What Cuba has is not what America wants or desires, no matter how enticing your political party makes it sound. This is evidenced by the tens of thousands who try to escape Cuba every year. A socialist state is something to be rid of and flee from. Free enterprise versus socialism—you can clearly see why Cubans want to come to America. Satan paints a similar picture to a vast number of people across this world. He says, "Let me dictate your life, and you will have everything you need." It is only a trap of the enemy of your soul, and once you are in that trap, you are powerless and can only have what he says you can have.

There is freedom in giving your heart and life to Jesus Christ. There is freedom in living a life, knowing that your heavenly Father will supply all your needs, according to His riches in glory. Free in Christ Jesus or a prisoner of Satan's regime? Freedom or imprisonment? It's a clear choice. Choose Jesus.

June 3

A New Season

Psalm 22:2

For the past few days, springtime in the midwestern Plains is up to its usual weather tactics: violent thunderstorms, wind, hail, tornados, snow on the eastern slope of Colorado, and feet of snow blanketing the mountains in late May. Old Man Winter does not give up easily, and the transition to summer takes several tries before it becomes reality.

Life often mimics nature. Transitions are sometimes met with an unwillingness to change. We would get bored with the same season all year long and welcome the change of seasons. Life consists of seasons of change. Like the weather, we don't just flip a page, and instantly it is summer. Our lives will encounter some blasts from the past as we move forward into new seasons. When that happens, we clean up fallen debris, find the shovel and clean the sidewalk, haul the broken limbs away, and prepare for the new season that awaits us.

Are you experiencing a new season in life? Embrace it.

June 4

Help Is Available

John 14:17

I'm a macho man, and I believe I can do a lot of things by myself. I have certainly entered into some things with enthusiasm, only to find out that I had not considered the full extent of what I was in for.

We are having some work done on our home. The macho me seriously considered doing it myself—and I could have. I just calculated that the work the construction crew had done in demolition, getting ready to start the project, would have taken me two weeks to accomplish, and the total project would have taken an enormous amount of time. I'm glad for the wisdom of my wife, who said, "You can't do it all by yourself."

I'm finding that God often comes to me in like manner and says, "You can't do it all by yourself." One of the functions of God's Holy Spirit is to come along beside us and help us. I am thankful for His help, and I'm thankful for construction crews that can get the job done quickly. Now I can use my Paid Time Off to do something less taxing.

June 5

All I Need

Exodus 3:11–15

It's an amazing thought that in my unlovable and deplorable state, God loves me. In my life of unforgiveness, God forgives me. In my sinfulness, He chooses to bear my sin. In my darkness, He becomes my light. In my despair, God becomes my hope. In my sickness, He is my healing. In my pitifulness, He picks me up. In my weakness, He is strength. In my brokenness, God is my restorer. In my need, God becomes my fulfillment. In my separation from God, He becomes my bridge to Him through Christ Jesus. God says of Himself, "I AM THAT I AM." Whatever God needs to be in my life, God already *is*. I don't have to wait while He creates that position and then fills it. He already *is*. Lesson for today: Let God be who He is—I AM.

June 6

News or Good News

1 Thessalonians 3:6–10

Part of the responsibility of our walk with Jesus is to spread the good news of the gospel. We live in a culture where lots of news is spread, but very little of it is "good" news. You may have read several news stories today, including bad news. Someone has died, or has an illness, misfortune, failure, and all sorts of news to get you down. Some good news gets passed around, and that's good, but it seems little of that pertains to the good news of the gospel that we are to share with the world around us.

Do you see how easy it is to share negative news? I have just done so here to this point. If we belong to Jesus, as one to whom He has granted salvation, then our responsibility is to share the good news—the news of what Jesus has done, what He is doing now, and by faith, what He is going to do tomorrow and in the future. In a world that thrives on news, I want to be sure that the good news is spread across the world and that my contribution is worthwhile and is considered good news.

June 7

Itchy Ears

2 Timothy 4:1–4

Our world today is plagued with a culture of "itchy ears." There seems to be a burning desire to hear the latest news of wrongdoing, failure, greediness, dark sins uncovered, and negativity that breeds even more of itself. We become what we hear, and filling our lives with negativity will create a negative attitude within.

God's command to His church, born-again Christians, is to bear good news, share the gospel, build one another up, and bear one another's burdens.

Yes, we will hear bad and negative news. My response must be of one who seeks good news, and I will fill my life with that. Let my ears "itch" for the good news of the gospel, and let my mouth (and writing) be full of words that build each of us up in Christ Jesus.

June 8

Procrastination—A Day of Reckoning

Ecclesiastes 11:4

I was awakened early this morning with a desire to accomplish a task that I'd put on hold for a while. It's one of those procrastination issues that is common in life. Sometimes the deadlines of completion overpower the motto of putting off until tomorrow what you don't want to do today. For me, tomorrow has arrived, and if I want to enjoy some free time with family over the Christmas holiday, then I must complete this task.

Many living their lives in Christ have a similar situation. God has given each of us tasks, and sometimes it is human nature to put off a task until another time. The task still waits as our procrastination takes priority. Sometimes God plants a task to do in our hearts; sometimes He assigns a task through someone else, perhaps a pastor, teacher, friend, or fellow worker. So today, I got up, got ready, and am working toward completion of the task before me. It's a God-given task, and I know He will help me.

If God has given you a task, and, like me, you have procrastinated, let me encourage you to let the end of this year be a catalyst to start and finish the task. If it's a God-given task, He will be faithful to help.

June 9

So What?

1 Kings 3:8–10

So what? It's an easy statement to make when we have a don't-care attitude. How am I to respond when people share something that is important to them? It's very subtle, but more and more, I detect that many people share inner and significant needs in the words they say and the way they say them. If I am careful, I can hear a different statement or question than what the words spoken might first reveal. I do not read minds, but I do hear the heart cry, if I but listen and think about what was shared for a moment. Many times in conversation, especially with family and friends, little hints are dropped of what is really happening in their lives while not exposing everything. Do I pry into their lives? Not unless I am absolutely certain that the Holy Spirit has directed me to do so—and that is a rarity. No, I take what I have heard and what I discern with my heart, and I bring it before the Lord God Almighty.

God's Word shares that as I pray in the Spirit, even with groaning and uttering that cannot be understood by humans, God understands, and my prayer to God is perfect, even though I do not understand the words or groaning.

Lord, take my so-what attitude and turn it into a listening heart that desires to see you work in the lives who have shared just a small portion of what they are going through. Amen.

Surprise!

1 Thessalonians 5:1–11

Surprise can consist of something good or something not so good, but surprise will always be—well, something of a surprise. I love when my grandkids try to surprise me with a gift or deed. I enjoy the times that I have pleasantly been surprised by an outcome or happening. I certainly don't enjoy the surprise of an unexpected bill cropping up, or a major appliance suddenly needing replacement, or a sudden death in the family. Our lives are filled with surprises, and the element of the unexpected seems to be a continual factor in our lives. Just think how boring life would be if there were no surprises. God's Word gives us clear understanding that a moment is coming when Jesus will instantly remove His waiting bride from this earth. The Bible is also very clear that Jesus is coming back to this earth a second time in power and glory, but with both events, there will be an element of surprise. Both events will catch many off guard and unprepared.

We often hear that we will probably be surprised at who we see and who we don't see as a part of these events. Don't let what God has promised to do in these two events catch you totally by surprise. Be ready. Jesus is preparing to take His bride home with Him. Jesus is coming back to earth a second time with such power that mountains will split, and the earth will quake. I'm getting ready to be involved in these two events.

June 11

You Are Not Forgotten

Isaiah 4:8–16

God desires for you to know that He has not forgotten you. Your tears have fallen to the floor and have puddled among the many prayers that you have spoken, only for you to feel that they have just fallen to the floor to lie among the tears. All the while, God seemingly stands by doing nothing, seemingly ignoring your circumstance. God seems inactive as your prayers and tears collect in significant amounts around you.

God's Word says that Jesus experiences every pain and circumstance we go through. In fact, He is touched and moved by how we feel, and He has more compassion than can be comprehended. You know this, but God seems to be sitting idly by, seemingly uncaring and unmoving. God says to you this day to put your complete trust, faith, and confidence in Him. At the proper time, He will respond in miraculous power and victory.

Your prayers are heard, each one, each time. Your tears have been collected in a bottle; that's how precious they are to God. Your situation is not too hard for Him to handle or too difficult to completely eliminate. I cannot tell you whether it will happen immediately or later, but God is going to do something powerful in your life. Keep trusting in God to do that. If He doesn't do it today, expect Him to do it tomorrow.

June 12

Your Attention, Please

Proverbs 14:34

The earth in Mexico quakes, the Atlantic Ocean froths with fury, the Gulf Coast of America is pounded with winds and floods, there are fires in the western US, and nature continues to groan. *Attention, please.* Millions need help, but our priority must be to sense what God is doing and saying through these disasters. I think it's simple: God wants our attention, and when He has our attention, then we must pursue righteousness. God's Word declares that righteousness exalts a nation. As a nation and a culture, we have embraced unrighteousness, providing a sanctuary for it and its followers. A continuation of following that path of unrighteousness will only bring destruction to our beloved nation. Righteousness is the only way this nation will ever be exalted by God Almighty. Righteousness starts here with you and me. It must start today, not tomorrow, next week, or next year—today.

June 13

Well, Are You Going to Answer Me?

Matthew 7:7

There is only *one* God, and He is God Almighty. I personally know Him as a God who listens and also speaks. I find myself, at times, treating God as only a listening God, when, in fact, there is unlimited power when He speaks. I find myself quickly expressing my needs, thanks, needs of others, and much more, then rushing headlong into my busy day. Unfortunately, I didn't take my turn in listening to God speak. Now I know that God's attributes and personality go far beyond my human capabilities and understanding, but I have a bit of an understanding of conversation between friends.

My closest human friend is my wife, LaDonna. We have been in conversation for well over fifty years now. Our earliest communication was by letter via postal service. We would ask each other questions and would wait until we received the letter, then respond with a letter. Sometimes there was almost a two-week interval before we would get the answers to our questions. We later experienced landline phone conversations, then email, then cell phones, and now text messages and Facebook. After all of this, surely we can read each other's minds. In some cases, yes, but most of the time, voiced communication remains the primary way of knowing our needs and desires and sharing information. Sometimes, a few moments after LaDonna asks me a question, she then asks, "Well, are you going to answer me?" In conversation, a response to the person who has just spoken is expected.

Don't cut God off short. He desires to speak. Give Him the opportunity to do so. There is not very much, if any, power in the petitions I bring before God. But when He speaks, all power in heaven and earth is at His command. Speak, Lord God Almighty. I am listening.

June 14

The Dream—It's Part of the Plan

1 Peter 3:1–7; Ephesians 6:1–4

It is very typical for young girls, teenagers, and even as women in adulthood to dream about their future in a perfect family—a mommy and daddy and babies. This dream is something that God has instilled. It was God's plan that young girls dream these dreams and focus on these thoughts. Fascination with marriage, babies, and complete families comes naturally to young girls. I am not trying to stereotype; it's just a personal observation. Young boys dream differently. They dream of following in Daddy's or Grandpa's footsteps or becoming firemen, or army soldiers, or cowboys. Being a daddy and having babies was something boys did only to play the roles when their sisters or a neighbor girl wanted to play house—and it quickly got boring. For boys, focusing on marriage, family, and babies occurs much later, sometimes not until the thirty's and beyond

My point is this: what kind of example are we portraying to our children and grandchildren to support wholesome, biblically defined families—Mommy, Daddy, and babies all living together in harmony? Our culture has made it easy to leave a marriage—too easy. Our culture has accepted that a marriage partner can be unfaithful, unloving, and hurtful, when God's Word says that is wrong. Whether you are at an age of just dreaming about a perfect marriage, just entering that perfect marriage, well down the road of that wonderful, near-perfect marriage, or struggling with a not-so-perfect marriage, make God the center of these dreams and relationships. Then and only then will you find the success and fulfillment of the God-given dreams of a mommy, a daddy, and babies. It's God's perfect plan—and it is enjoyable!

June 15

Who's to Blame

Matthew 7:1–5

I am to blame. That's a statement very seldom heard in our culture today. Instead, we say "you" are to blame, or we place blame as far away from us as possible. Today's news (late 2017) is filled with blaming the Russians for interfering with our November elections. There is plenty of blame in our culture today, but no one accepts any part of it. It's popular to direct blame onto unsuspecting individuals, just to watch them squirm and try to set themselves free from the blame by passing it on to someone else. Throwing blame on someone else is a learned behavior in our culture at an early age. Toddlers, as innocent as they are, will place blame for something they did wrong on someone or something else. That is just the start of what we see as a significant pattern in our world today.

Taking ownership of blame takes a strong man or woman who, with the help of God, recognizes that placing blame elsewhere is wrong and a sin against God. For America to become great again, men and women, young people, and boys and girls will need to shoulder blame, pay the consequences, and live lives of integrity. Let's end the "blame game." God would be pleased with that.

June 16

Why Me, Lord?

2 Corinthians 12:7–10

Why me? Why did this happen to me? Why, out of all the people in the world, do I have to experience this?

I have several friends, family, and loved ones who ask themselves those questions (and at times, I do so myself). I wish I could take them by their hands, peer into their eyes, and tell them specifically why they are going through what they are experiencing. The truth is, I do not know, and the only one who does know, Jesus Christ, is keeping the answer to Himself for the moment.

For those who are asking those questions today, I offer this from God's Word:

> In his kindness God called you to share in his eternal glory by means of Christ Jesus. So, after you have suffered a little while, he will restore, support, and strengthen you, and he will place you on a firm

> foundation. All power to Him forever. Amen. (1 Peter 5:10–11 NLT)

I trust in the God who has all power to restore, support, and strengthen you, and place you on a firm foundation. Faith is not dependent on circumstances. My circumstances are dependent on my faith and patience in knowing that the one who started a good work in me will be faithful and complete it. Be encouraged. There is restoration, support, strength, and firm footing ahead. That is a promise from God.

June 17

Knock-Knock—Who's There?

Revelation 3:20

Doorbells are a convenience in our modern world. During our house renovation, we have been without a doorbell, and visitors have had to knock on the door to get our attention. We will soon have the doorbells reinstalled, but can I say that a knock on the door was refreshing.

In the book of Revelation, John shares these words of Jesus: "Behold, I stand at the door and knock" (Revelation 3:20). Jesus desires to visit you—right where you are. No matter where you are or how messy your life is, Jesus is knocking at the door of your life at this moment. It's a simple task—open the door, and let Jesus in.

By the way, He brings gifts—salvation, peace, joy, comfort, healing, restoration, and much more. He is patiently knocking at your life's door. Go ahead. Let Jesus in today.

Unwavering God

Malachi 3:1–6

In reading the Chronological Bible, it's interesting to note that before John wrote the revelation of Jesus Christ, the apostles' last messages to the church and the world at large was this: Watch out for false prophets, be careful not to waver from faith in Jesus Christ, and flee from sin.

I am convinced that God Almighty is an unwavering God and does not change. Those things that He called sin thousands of years ago are still sin today. And those things He called righteous are still righteous today. In our culture today, there is a subtle but strong and fast-moving trend to water down God's Word, sugar-coat false teachings, and accept any belief as being equal to God's Word. God's Word is the final authority. My changing it to fit my lifestyle or accepting others' change to fit their lifestyles is simply unaccepted by God. God's church here on earth will be bombarded with false teaching, much of which will be presented in an inviting and enticing manner; it will appear attractive. The only way servants of the living God can discern false teaching is to know the Word of God.

Read the Word. It is *truth.* And it will set you free—and keep you free.

June 19

Hear the Warning; Heed the Warning

Revelation 3:18–22

The book of Revelation is intriguing, to say the least. It is full of information regarding end times for this world as we know it. The book reveals much about the calamity, death, and destruction that will occur during a relatively short period. Most theologians would agree that we are fast approaching the time that is described as John recorded it in the book of Revelation. Will those who have received Jesus Christ as their salvation and Savior and who still are living on earth experience any of the terrors outlined in these writings? I do not know; no one but God the Father Himself knows when He will take His children out of this earth.

Personally, I believe that God's church—those who are saved—will be caught up to heaven before these terrors take place. What if I am wrong, and the church remains here on earth during that time? From my viewpoint, the only way anyone could survive what will take place is by knowing Jesus as Lord and Savior. The need of salvation is real. Each of us needs God's salvation through Jesus Christ today.

I don't know the specifics of tomorrow, but a time is coming soon when each of us will be glad that we know Jesus as Savior and Lord. Don't let the trickery of the enemy of your soul lead you to abandon your salvation. Jesus is my Lord and Savior, and I am thankful.

A Tree of Life

Genesis 3:22–24; Revelation 22:1–21

God's Word records information about a tree of life in both the first and last books of God's holy Word. In Genesis, the tree of life grows in the garden of Eden, and in Revelation, it is part of what Jesus reveals as a significant part of heaven. I believe the meaning of the tree of life is self-explanatory, but I want to address the significance of the tree of life.

In the garden, Adam and Eve were told not to eat of the fruit of both the tree of knowledge and the tree of life. Sin entered this world when they ate from the tree of knowledge, and Adam and Eve were removed from the garden. In heaven, the fruit from the tree of life appears to be freely eaten. The fear of eternal death, torment, and separation from eternal God scares the whey out of me. The concept and knowledge of eternal Life in the presence of a holy God is very attractive and persuades me to make sure of my salvation through Jesus Christ.

I love most fruit, and I am certain I will love the fruit of the tree of life in heaven. In hell, amid all the pain and torment that is eternal, there will be no time or desire for eating. There will only be an intense desire for water that is not available. Not only that, but there is indication that worms will feed on the eternally damned bodies—worms that never die. Salvation or hopelessness—which shall it be? I choose salvation and the tree of life in God's heaven.

June 21

Abba Father

Romans 8:14–17

On this Father's Day, my earthly father is celebrating with the heavenly Father. While I would certainly welcome one more time to see and talk to my dad, I would not want him to leave the presence of our heavenly Father. Someday, I too will join them, and what a glorious day that will be. Until then, my assignment is to be an earthly father to my children and grandchildren. I believe the grandkids enjoy being where I am and being with me because they constantly ask to stay or go with me. It was the same for me with my grandfather. My grandpa was always doing something that I wanted to participate in. I enjoyed spending time with him. He also is in heaven, celebrating Father's Day with my dad and the heavenly Father. To my heavenly Father and to all the father figures in my life who are spending this Father's Day with the heavenly Father, I miss you and look forward to that time when we will be together again. Happy Father's Day.

June 22

Moving from Glory to Glory

2 Corinthians 3:12–18

It was everything that we had hoped it would be. The beach had wonderful sand. The water was warm, from the Gulf Stream. The weather was sunny and warm, and we had a delightful few minutes in which we enjoyed what God had put together for us. But then it was time to move on. We would have enjoyed staying there all afternoon, but we were scheduled to be at another location later in the day.

In the journey of life, we often hit memorable times and wish that we could spend more time in those moments. But life goes on, and we have another place we must be. I am thankful that God, who knows what lies in my path today and every day, directs my path. I love those wonderful times that God places in my path, but I also recognize that He has a further destination laid out for me. It may be a road strewn with large boulders rather than a sandy beach, but that's OK because I know God walks with me. And He's OK with my holding His hand when the path gets rough. Just hold God's hand and go where He wants you to go today.

June 23

Called to Change

Matthew 4:18–22

I find it amazing how God will change the course of life in short order. As I read the Gospels' account of Jesus calling the fishermen to become disciples, I saw that the men were having a normal day of work. They had spent the night fishing and now they were drying and repairing their nets. It was a normal day; then came Jesus. Jesus simply said, "Follow Me," and they immediately left their livelihood without so much as packing a bag and followed Jesus. Mary was having a normal day, doing her chores and normal routine and probably thinking about preparation for her upcoming wedding to Joseph. Then came God's messenger, and her life was never the same.

Most of us this week have a normal routine planned. I do, and planning is a good thing. But don't be surprised if your routine is interrupted by God with a change to your course. Routine activity is an open invitation for God to stop by and say, "Follow Me."

June 24

Walking with God

Deuteronomy 5:32–33

We are at a hotel near a beautiful beach on the Gulf Coast this morning—pure white sand, glistening water, and gentle waves. The beach is very inviting—many miles long, with plenty of room for thousands of people. Today, the beach is empty and devoid of people. The attraction of the lovely beach has been overwhelmed by near-freezing temperatures, and folks have chosen to not be here. The beach is just as beautiful and inviting as on a hot summer day, but no one is interested.

The things of God are like the beach situation today. We desire to be involved when things are perfect, in our perspective, but if the "weather" turns a little chilly, we crawl into our secure place and do not participate in what God has prepared for us. Just think where this world would be if Moses and the children of Israel had not stepped into the great sea because the wind was blowing too hard. Yep, sometimes God wants us to walk with Him, even if the weather is not the most desirable.

June 25

Nonadjustable

Acts 4:5–12

Adjustment is a normal part of life. I find myself very comfortable as I drift off to sleep in my bed each night, but I wake up several times in the night to adjust to a different position. The seat in my work truck is adjustable, and I often take advantage of adjusting the seat to fit my comfort level. Summer has hit this weekend, and I have adjusted the thermostat accordingly. But there is an area that I refuse to adjust, and that is my salvation. The world wants me to water it down and compromise, but God tells us in His Word that those things are not pleasing or acceptable to Him.

Adjusting the belt loop I use is fine, but adjusting God's salvation to fit the world's definition is totally unacceptable.

Saved only by God's grace and not of my own works. No adjustment needed.

June 26

Is God Speaking?

Job 33:12–14

I've often heard people say, "I don't seem to be hearing anything from God." My simple reply is, "Read His Word." God's Word is a message designed by God to speak plainly and clearly to everyone on an individual basis, as well as corporately. If you feel that it's been a while since you heard from God, open His Word and let Him speak to you. God speaks directly and openly about His love and forgiveness, His mercy, and His grace. God has something significant and specific to say to you today. Let God do it through His Word. Open your Bible, and let God speak.

You Don't Want to be in This Hailstorm

Revelation 16:21

God's Word gives us descriptions of some very large things, some of which I want to enjoy and some of which I want no part of. About 3:30 this morning, a good old-fashioned Plains thunderstorm passed through the area. It began with a tremendous lightning show as it approached, and then, as the leading edge came overhead, it dropped hailstones—a lot of them. Some stones were the size of ping-pong balls and caused damage to roofs, cars, and buildings. The largest recorded measurement of a hailstone was in 2010; it was roughly the size of a volleyball and weighed just under two pounds. Quite small when compared to the hailstorm described in Revelation, in which hailstones weighed more than seventy-five pounds. The diameter would be greater than twenty inches and would have fallen to earth at well over 350 miles per hour, if just dropping from the sky. Who knows how fast they will be traveling if God's angel hurls them at the earth?

Two things are required to create the hailstones that occurred in our weather today: (1) cloud vapor that reaches up to seventy thousand feet into the sky, where the temperature is greater than minus-sixty degrees Fahrenheit, and (2) high-velocity winds capable of lifting raindrops and ice repeatedly, until the weight becomes too heavy and drops to the ground as hail. I have heard the winds howl in the upper atmosphere as this is happening, and it is a frightful experience, just to hear those winds blow.

Imagine the amount of wind and wind speed needed to build a seventy-five-pound hailstone. Certainly, it would be a magnitude never experienced prior to the event described in Revelation. Imagine the damage and destruction that would occur from seventy-five-pound–plus hailstones. Very few structures or vehicles could withstand such a happening. If I observe this event—and it will happen because it is God's Word—I want to observe it from the balconies of heaven. Yes, God has great wrath planned to punish those who are not saved, but He also has great blessing for those who are saved. I choose blessing.

June 28

Walls—Defense or Offense

2 Chronicles 14:6–7

Walls have a dual purpose—keeping in and keeping out. During winter, walls of homes keep us warm inside, while keeping the cold outside. Sometimes in life, we refer to those who have built walls around themselves as unsociable. They are not outgoing and don't let anyone into their lives. If we don't know the details, we often wonder what horrific tragedy must have occurred in their lives to cause them to build such walls.

Certainly, building personal walls to keep bad influences out is a desired building project, but walling everyone out has a profound, negative impact on the person building the wall and those around him or her. If you have built a wall around yourself, I would encourage you to open the door and invite Jesus into your life. He can mend the pieces that caused you to build the wall, and He can help you to open the door for others to come into your life. You were made to be a social being. Start with letting Jesus into your entire life. That's the start of many great things to come.

June 29

Where Is My Faith?

Luke 8:22–25

Where is your faith? It was a question Jesus asked the disciples after He had calmed the wind and waves on a stormy sea. Many of the disciples were seasoned fishermen and accustomed to stormy weather, but with this storm, they were afraid they would all drown. Jesus, worn out from ministering all day, was comfortably sleeping in the back of the boat until the disciples woke Him in their fear and panic. I know the feeling of being awakened from a deep and much-needed sleep. Whatever the cause for awakening me better be very important, and I'm probably going to be abrupt with any response. I sense the abruptness of Jesus, as He immediately rebukes the wind and waves. I sense the tone of His voice when He asks, "Where is your faith?"

Before Jesus ascended into heaven, He told His followers—and us as well—that He would give us power to do all the things that He did while living among humans and even greater things. I believe that Jesus is still asking that same question: "Where is your faith?"

Lord God Almighty, my simple request is that my personal faith in You would be adequate to meet the needs that will come before me.

Where is your faith? For me, it's a personal question that stirs an intense desire to be certain I have enough faith and to know that I do.

Transfer of Burden

Matthew 11:28–30

One of my most favorite verses in God's Word is found in Matthew:

> Then Jesus said, "Come to me, all of you who are weary and carry heavy burdens, and I will give you rest. Take my yoke upon you. Let me teach you, because I am humble and gentle at heart, and you will find rest for your souls. For my yoke is easy to bear, and the burden I give you is light." (Matthew 11:28–30 NLT)

Burden-bearing is not one of those sought-after things of life. If possible, we will move away from them. But burdens are a fact of life; some are great, and some are small. Burdens can be identified in almost everything. Guilt, pain, suffering, sin, family, health, finances, and sorrow are just a few of the burdens many people carry in life today. This promise of Jesus, God's Son, is for everyone who is burdened today. You give the heavy burden to Him, and Jesus gives you a light burden. Yes, it is that simple.

Sometimes I choose to continue with the heavy burden instead of exchanging it for a lighter one. Why? My pride says I can handle the load, and I choose to not give the burden to Jesus. But He waits patiently and willingly accepts my burden when I am willing to give it to Him.

So, you are carrying a heavy burden today. Don't make Jesus shake His head in wonder while He has His arms stretched out toward you. It's simple; just give your burden to the Lord, and leave it there.

July 1

Eternity—A Numbers Game for Humans

1 Peter 3:8

Today marks the halfway point in the year. My, where does the time go? While time quickly passes before us and moves past us, God tells us that in heaven, a thousand years will be as a day. In the light of eternity, these 180 days that we have experienced since January 1 would be as 180,000 years. Let that settle in your mind a bit. In a couple of weeks, I will turn sixty-nine years old—that's 25.185 million years in heaven's equation. Evangelist and singer Larry Lundstrom (Larry Lundstrom Ministries) sings this line from an old song: "The first million years will find me sitting round the feet of the Lord." Eternity in heaven—the numbers are beyond our comprehension. Time won't matter, and never again will I be late or early.

July 2

A Declaration of Independence

John 8:31–36

Independence and Independence Day for the United States is a big deal. It was with wisdom asked of God by the men who came together in 1776, and God granted that wisdom and direction, and a Declaration of Independence was written. That was the easy part. These same men and an army of volunteers had to then win that independence, with many giving their lives for what we enjoy today. Freedom is not free, whether we are talking about our nation's independence or our independence from sin.

If you are battling life-controlling issues, your freedom already has been won at the cross of Jesus Christ. Rather than living for our freedom, Jesus died for it. And then He defeated death and lives again. The declaration of independence for your life-controlling issues has already been written. There are battles yet to be won, but the declaration has been made. Independence is yours. Now fight for it, in Jesus's name. Believe me; it's worth it and worth a celebration when the victory is won. Happy Fourth of July, everyone.

July 3

America—Founded on Freedom to Worship God

1 Chronicles 16:23–33

This week, the USA celebrates its birthday once again. Tons of fireworks will be set off in a brilliant display of Independence Day. I am thankful for past generations that were willing to sacrifice their lives to gain the freedom to start a new life in a new land. Predominant in their desire to settle in America was an ability to openly worship the one and only true God and to openly gather in worship without fear of reprisal. Much has happened since that time, but this Sunday, we will worship in our church the one and true living God. We will do so without fear of reprisal. My appreciation swells for those who were visionary in their pursuit of happiness to include my freedom of worship to the one and true living God. Join me in worship as a part of our celebration.

July 4

Independence—A Driving Force

Psalm 33:12

In 1776, men from North America gathered together and, on July 4, signed the Declaration of Independence. July 4 of every year is known as Independence Day in the United States. A major driving force that led to the signing of the Declaration of Independence was a common view that there had to be freedom to worship God in a manner that was pleasing to Him. This driving and compelling force was a major influence in the fighting and winning of America's independence.

There is a vast need in the heart of America for men and women to rise up and worship God as He intended individuals to worship Him. There is a vast need for the heart of America to turn itself back to God and worship Him in reverence and in fear. There must arise in America a people who will not only stand up for godly values but will also stand in the place of representation in leadership for this great nation. If godly men and women do not stand up in leadership and representation of this nation, then the ungodly will do so.

Independence from ungodly leadership and representation is still worth fighting for.

July 5

Divided

Romans 16:17–19

My travels take me past many historical points of interest across this great nation. I do not have time to stop at all of them, but when I can, I stop and read a brief history at a monument erected alongside the road. Many of these places were battlefields in our nation's history. The Civil War battlefields are of most interest to me because our nation was nearly equally divided in its view of being for or against slavery. In many cases, families were divided, and, in many battles, brother fought against brother.

Our nation today reminds me of the opposing views that brought a Civil War to this nation some 160 years ago. Today, our nation is near equally divided on many social issues, as well as political and world issues, and it's evident in national elections over the past few years. Most issues that divide our country can be characterized as being opposed to God's Word or supporting God's Word. For America, there is a clear path to either God's favor or God's righteous judgment. God's Word gives clarity of God's position on many personal and social issues that our world faces today.

Let's take our social and personal issues and lay them out beside God's Word. Do you desire God's judgment? Then continue to support personal and social issues that are clearly going against the Word of God. Do you want God's favor? Then let's align our personal lives and social issues with God's Word. That's the battlefield of today. How will history record what took place on this battlefield? As for me and my household, we choose the Lord. Any other choice, and we would end in defeat.

July 6

A Large Crowd

Revelation 19:1–8

There are a lot of comments about the size of crowds at various functions in our current culture. I am glad to be numbered with the crowd that is without number, and that crowd is the blood-bought throng. I don't have to march through streets of large cities because my Redeemer walks on streets of pure gold. I don't have to wave a billboard-sized sign because everything I need to share with others is recorded in God's holy Word. I don't have to travel thousands of miles to join others. I can walk into my church and join with many others in proclaiming Jesus to our world. The world identifies with large masses of people bringing about change, yet it was one person, Jesus Christ, who revolutionized the world with His Word, His life, His death, and His resurrection.

I am a crowd of one. There resides in me a faith to move mountains, part the sea, make a crooked path straight, heal the sick, raise the dead, and set the captive free.

Lord God Almighty, let that kind of faith arise in our individual hearts and lives today, and then may it be loosed in Jesus's name. May our individual march be one of victory. Lord God, guide my steps today as I continue my march in holiness. Let mighty faith arise in my life to accomplish what You want to accomplish. In the mighty name of Jesus.

July 7

The Mighty Hand of God

Matthew 8:1–4

God's Word shares that nearly everywhere Jesus went during His three years of ministry, He was met by the sick, lame, diseased, blind, deaf, demon-possessed, and countless others who needed healing and deliverance that only Jesus could provide. Never once do we see anyone walk away without getting the healing or deliverance for which they had come to Jesus. In fact, many times God's Word declares that Jesus healed them all. God's Word declares that Jesus Christ is the same yesterday, today, and forever. If Jesus healed and delivered them all then, He can certainly do it today.

Lord God, our healer and our deliverer, so many of us are standing, sitting, kneeling, lying, or running before You, their healer, their deliverer, seeking Your touch and Your deliverance at this very moment. Will You turn away? Will You not respond? Will You not reach out Your mighty hand in healing power and deliverance this very moment? Let mighty faith arise within us that we might see the mighty hand of God accomplish healing and deliverance today, in Jesus's name.

July 8

Contagious

1 Corinthians 14:12

God desires that His people quit sitting by, hoping for Him to do something. He desires for His children to be fully involved in what He is doing.

If I am going to spend eternity with God, doing all that He has planned for me in heaven, should I not start here in this life, by involving myself in what He is doing on earth?

Let excitement return to the people of God. Let zeal be a trademark of living for Jesus. May our enthusiasm for Jesus be more contagious, more infectious, and more widespread than any communicable diseases present in our world.

Live for Jesus—and give it all you've got!

July 9

Operator Control
1 Corinthians 10:11–13

Once again, our news is filled with results of terrorist actions, this time using a large truck and firing a gun while driving into a large crowd of people celebrating a festive holiday in France. I've written about the inanimate objects that can be used in killing and maiming other humans. Obviously, that includes every inanimate object that someone could pick up or move through technology, as well as trucks, planes, and trains. Traveling as I do, I pass tens of thousands of trucks on the road each year. Sometimes there are accidents, some of which are caused by mechanical malfunction, but most all the time, those trucks were under full control of the driver.

The driver steers the truck and guides its course. From reports at the scene in Nice, France, it was the truck driver who inflicted the violence. He had both a gun and a truck at his disposal. But it was the driver's will that caused the deaths of many. Only when the heart of an individual can be changed to love rather than hate will we see a decrease in incidents like this. Only Jesus can remove the hate and replace it with love—His love. Any religion that promotes hate is not of almighty God and must be called out as such. Let the love of God Almighty overcome any other god that promotes hate and fear.

July 10

Expectation
Philippians 1:18–21

Today is a day of expectation, although we could say the same about every day. I watched the weather report last night, and I expect it to get hot again today (over one hundred degrees). I can expect the mail to be delivered somewhere close to two o'clock. I can expect a phone call around 9:15 this morning to give me a time for a meeting later today. Our lives are full of expectation.

As people who serve God, we should have daily expectations as well. I expect (and know) that God will hear me when I communicate with Him. I can expect God to respond when I am in His presence. When I ask of God for wisdom in business or family matters, I can expect that God will give wisdom. When I ask His help, I can expect that He will help me. Too many Christians go through their daily routine without expectation of God doing something marvelously wonderful in their lives today. God has something good in store for me today, and I have expectation.

July 11

A Solid Platform

Psalm 18:1–3

Platforms are a needed element in the world around us. Platforms provide a solid base from which to launch, build, or speak. Many wind turbines are being constructed in our area. Some of these reach three hundred feet into the sky with the fan blades and stand ready to generate energy from the nearly constant wind here. The base of these towers is anchored to a concrete platform that is quite large and goes many feet into the ground. This platform provides stability even in the hurricane-force winds that sometimes accompany storms.

Those running for political office often refer to the platform of their designated party, indicating that what they propose will align with that platform. Pastors, preachers, and evangelists preach the Word of God from the platform that is a place of solidness to speak forth the Word of God. As our world rushes headlong into biblical last days, it will be vital to have a solid platform on which to live and stand. There is no better platform than God Almighty and Jesus Christ, His Son, and the Word of God. I openly question the value and soundness of many things that are included in the political platforms. But I openly declare that the platform of the Lord, my God, is solid and without flaw. On Christ, the solid rock, I stand.

July 12

Gone

1 John 1:7-9

Gone. *Gone.* G-o-n-e. That's what has happened to my sins. God's Word tells us that when God forgives us of our sins, He buries them in a deep sea of forgetfulness. God will never bring them before His throne again. As a human, I live in a place where warfare occurs in the spiritual realms. A Holy God plans for my future, forgetting my past. The enemy of my soul desires that I look back as he dredges up all the sins of my past. I have watched as river barges have worked to dredge channels in rivers. All they do is bring up muck and stir up the water. That's what the enemy of our souls does best—stirs up the muck and the mire and dirties the water. Jesus gives refreshing life-giving water of life.

My life is in you, Lord. I want the refreshing, life-giving water that flows from Your throne. The muck and the mire are buried. It's *gone*!

July 13

Blemish Corrected

1 Peter 1:13–25

It's just a small thing. It won't be a problem.

It started as a hairline crack in our kitchen sink—very small and not leaking. That was several months ago. Now the crack has widened and is leaking water. I have just repaired it with an epoxy that I hope will keep it from leaking. We didn't catch that it was leaking until it had soaked some boxes of soap that we had under the sink. Sometimes our Christian walk is similar—just a little blemish that doesn't cause any trouble. But left unrepaired, that blemish grows larger until it negatively impacts our lives and grows larger each day. The best choice is to fix it before it starts causing problems. And the best part is that God is willing to help fix it. And He is a professional at doing so. Don't you just love it when a professional gets on the job? The job is done right and quickly. He has all the needed tools and doesn't have to make several trips to the hardware store for supplies.

Lord God, fix my life in the areas that need repair.

July 14

Knowing the Voice of God

Jeremiah 33:3

I want to express my gratitude to all who took time to wish me a happy birthday. I count it as a blessing to receive these notes and various pictures and attachments. Thank you for making my day special. LaDonna, Jolyn, and family fixed me a wonderful meal last evening and a cake laden with way too many candles, some of which didn't stop burning no matter how often I blew them out. I hope my life is like those candles, and the fire keeps burning.

You may sense that God is speaking to you, yet you are unclear about what to do with that. How does God—the great and almighty God of everything known and unknown—speak to us? God created humans, and in doing so, our Creator God wove into our beings—physical, emotional, spiritual, and relational—an ability to hear and understand what God is saying to us. At times, we may be unable to fully comprehend all that He is speaking to us, but we can know with assurance that God is speaking.

You may ask, "How do I know it is God?" As much as I would like for God to appear before me and speak audible words to me, that has never happened and probably will not until I am in heaven. I do not know that God has even spoken in an audible voice to me, but I know, beyond any shadow of doubt, that He speaks to me—and often.

Many voices try to get our attention, so how do we know that it is God? By getting to know Him and His heart. We can do that, in part, by reading His Word and communicating with God.

Surprise yourself. Today, carve out a set amount of time—thirty minutes would be a good start—and tell God that you are setting aside this time to hear from Him. Then open His Word, the Bible. (I enjoy the New Living Translation. You can choose from many different translations at biblegateway.com, a free app.) If you have not read much of God's Word on your own, I would suggest starting with John 1:1, and read the first three chapters. I would then encourage you to meditate on what you have read and ask God to speak to your open heart.

God often speaks in a still, small voice, which means that I must have an environment that is suitable for hearing that voice. I enjoy good Christian music, but sometimes God wants all my attention without interference. Then wait to hear from God. It may happen quickly, or it may happen after some time—perhaps the next day or days later. Sometimes God just wants to see how sincere we are in hearing from Him. Hearing from God is an important function of how God created us.

Perhaps you sense that God has spoken or is speaking to you, and you are struggling with what He is speaking into your life. Tell God just how you feel and the struggle you are having. Then wait to hear from God. Good things—God things—come to those who wait to hear from God. He is a personable God, and I know He wants to speak into your life today. Give Him time to do so.

July 15

Speaking Forth Wisdom

James 3:13–18

There have been many times in my life when I have received godly counsel from someone who was willing to speak to me in godly wisdom. Those times were opportunities to see myself from a different perspective and to make life-changing moves that would be pleasing to God. I am thankful for people who will, in wisdom, speak into my life in direction, correction, and motivation. I now find myself in a place of speaking wisdom into the lives of others as God gives me divine direction. I know and understand that I cannot and do not speak from a life of perfection, but I can speak from a heart of compassion and from a sense of God's Holy Spirit living in me.

Lord God Almighty, all wisdom is Yours. Help me today to speak wisdom into the hearts and lives of those I will speak to today. Amen.

July 16

One of a Kind

Mark 10:6-9

A one-of-a-kind object is a rarity that's often considered priceless. We may consider a one-of-a-kind object to be something like a painting, a car, a building or home, or perhaps a piece of jewelry or a gem. We greatly value and may desire such rare and priceless items.

As an individual, a human being, I was created as one of a kind. So were you. There are many of us, but each of us is a one-of-a-kind, and each one is precious to God, and to our spouses and families as well. The same applies to a marriage relationship. The two shall become one. This union is one of a kind—a treasure, a gem, a tapestry that is unique and not identical to any other.

Let me encourage you today to see yourself as God created you. A priceless, one-of-a-kind jewel that He values beyond price. Let me encourage you in your marriage to see the uniqueness of what God has done in taking two individuals, male and female, and creating one unique relationship that is priceless. Treat your marriage as the priceless, one-of-a-kind treasure that it is. A priceless life and a priceless marriage are not contingent upon volumes of money. They are contingent on how we treat each other. One of a kind—I'm rich in what I have in my life and my marriage. I have in my possession and I am part of one of a kind.

The Substance and Evidence of Faith

Hebrews 11:1

God's Word defines faith as something we get, in part, from reading and hearing God's Word. It's defined as the substance of things hoped for and the evidence of things not yet seen. When God created me, He knew that simplicity would be a key element for my complete understanding of some of the things of God. I have faced enough of life to know that I must possess the faith that is described in God's Word.

It is by faith that we are saved and forgiven of our sins. Somewhere in life, we realize that sin separates us from God and that we need God in our lives. By faith, we accept Jesus Christ, the Son of God, as our Savior, and we stand in righteousness before God Almighty because of what Jesus did in cleansing us from sin. As defined in scripture, faith is substance. It is real, and it has volume or size, as Jesus declares that faith the size of a mustard seed would move mountains into the sea.

Faith also has evidence. It has telltale signs; it leaves a trail of evidence. The proof is in the result. The woman who was healed of the issue of blood heard that Jesus the healer was nearby. Her faith was moved to the point of action, as she believed that if only she could touch the hem of Jesus's garment, she would be healed. Her healing was instantaneous and complete when she did touch Jesus's garment.

Where is my faith? It may mean that I might have to crawl through a crowd of people to touch Jesus. Jesus often asked people what they wanted from Him, and as they asked for specific healing, He healed them of all their diseases and illnesses. I desire a faith like that—a faith that can come only through God's Word and have substance and evidence.

Follow the Instructions

Luke 24:45–49

In Bible study last night, we were discussing the great commission and Jesus's instructions to His followers after He would go to heaven to be with His Father. His followers were told to go back to Jerusalem and wait until they were filled with the power of the Holy Spirit. We know now that the waiting period was days from Jesus's leaving this earth until the mighty outpouring of the Holy Ghost.

Something caught my attention last night. Jesus told His followers to go back to Jerusalem and wait there—the very city where Jesus had been arrested, beaten, and crucified and where the disciples had scattered because of the threats on their lives. Jesus sent them right back into the middle of the conflict. The memory was still fresh and potent of what had happened forty days earlier, but that is where Jesus sent them, not to some secluded place in the hills or by the shore. It was right in the middle of what was going on.

God says today that right now, in the middle of all the pressure and circumstance that surrounds you, do not run and hide, but shut yourself in with almighty God and the Son of God, Jesus Christ, until you are endowed with the power of the third equal person of the Trinity, the Holy Ghost. Then and only then will you be able to face in victory what the enemy of your soul has thrown in your path. We are overcomers because of the Word of God, which is our testimony, and the blood of the Lamb, which has been applied to our lives, and because of the power of the Holy Ghost. Right now, amid all the circumstances that surround you, make a place to wait until you have been given power —Holy Ghost power.

July 19

Truth or Lies

Psalm 19:14

Who is lying, and who is telling the truth? Every day our lives are bombarded with words. They come from family members, friends, the media, and a host of other sources. I join with the psalmist who says, "Let the words of my mouth and the meditation of my heart be pure before God" (Psalm 19:14). I have been lied to and absolutely knew it at the time the words were spoken. I have also been told the truth and knew beyond any doubt that it was so. Which do I appreciate, and which do I loathe? I appreciate the truth. How do I accept future words from someone who I know has lied to me in the past? Certainly, with skepticism at the very least.

I desire that my words are truthful and not questioned and certainly not lies.

Lord God Almighty, give me a heart of truth and a mouth that speaks truth always. And as I discern those who lie to me, may I flee from following in their paths. Why? Because God's Word says that liars have no place in heaven. That leaves only one option—hell. Lying is not for the Righteous.

By the way, God's Word does not distinguish between a "white lie" and any other. Lies are all classified the same—lies.

July 20

A Quiet Time

Psalm 46:10–11

I am writing this at a quiet hour of the day. The streets are empty, and businesses are still dark, and in a few minutes, I will hit the road for another busy week of work. The quietness and stillness offer a solitude moment that is free of busyness and hurriedness. It is a good time for reflection. As I consider the blessings of God, I realize that they far outweigh any trials or difficulty I have encountered. I am blessed beyond measure, blessed beyond worthiness.

Thank you, Lord God Almighty, for your blessings that you bestow upon me and my family. Father God, you are generous and kind. You are God, and I am thankful for Your salvation that you freely give. Blessings from You, oh Lord, start with Your salvation, and then they don't merely add up; they multiply. Thank you, God, for multiplied blessings.

July 21

Let Us Pray

Matthew 6:5–13

Great leaders exhibit great qualities. My Facebook newsfeed of February 2017 has several clips of First Lady Melania Trump leading a large crowd in Melbourne, Florida, in the Lord's Prayer. I have personally watched this clip and am struck by the humility and sincerity with which our First Lady simply said, "Let us pray." I'm pretty sure that most of the people attending this function had no thought beforehand that they would pray this prayer before the day was done, especially in a large crowd setting and with the First Lady leading. And as the end of the prayer approached, you could hear the voices of the crowd blending with Melania's, saying the Lord's Prayer in unison.

Praying the Lord's Prayer at public gatherings—what a novel idea. First Lady Melania, we take your lead and follow your incredible example.

Our Father, which art in heaven, hallowed be Thy name. Thy kingdom come; thy will be done in earth as it is in heaven. Give us this day our daily bread. And forgive us our debts as we forgive our debtors. And lead us not into temptation, but deliver us from evil. For Thine is the kingdom, and the power, and the glory forever. Amen.

July 22

Desperation Brings Us Close to God

Psalm 9:1–16

Desperation brings humanity to a place of crying out to God. God hears us in our desperation, but He also hears us at other times. Almighty God is not just a hearing God. He is also a listening God. He waits for us to speak to Him. I can visualize God in heaven, anticipating my song, my praise, my worship, my request, and my listening in return. Do I keep God waiting? I hope not. I know in my heart that God is waiting for my time with Him today. I am not in a desperate place today, but God gladly hears what I have to say. Don't let desperation be the only catalyst to bring you to God. Allow God's goodness and mercy to encourage you to spend time drawing near to our heavenly Father.

July 23

It Happened in My Lifetime

2 Timothy 3:1–5

When asked by His disciples what would be the sign of the end of the age, Jesus responded with several things that would take place. In my sixty-five years of life, I have been a witness to nearly everything that Jesus said would be the sign of the nearness of His return to earth. My life spans about 3.25 percent of the time since Jesus's birth, which introduced this age of grace dispensation). In that small amount of time, all the things Jesus said about the end of this age have come to pass, and it has been in my lifetime.

If I live to be eighty-three, I will have lived for 4 percent of the time since Jesus's birth. Four percent is mostly insignificant, but when it contains as much biblical prophecy being fulfilled as my life has seen, then I had better take notice. Jesus is coming back. And the signs of our times prove that the time is close. It is nearly the midnight hour. We must watch, we must be ready, and we must tell others. I'm ready to leave this world when God calls. It is nearly time—perhaps today.

July 24

Putting God's Tools to Work

1 Timothy 1:5–8

For a couple of days, I am helping to build an office for our research program in southwest Kansas. It is fun to break out the tools that have not been used for a while and put them to work again. God's Word declares that the kingdom of God is continually "under construction." Perhaps, in your normal routine, God will ask you to take out the tools that have been idle for a while and use them once again.

The feel of a hammer in my hand and holding lumber in place with the other still feels good. A nailer and drill-driver for screws are still fun to operate, and reading a tape measure and cutting boards and then nailing them together gives a sense of accomplishment that has been renewed again.

The apostle Paul told young Timothy to stir up the gifts that God had given to him at an even earlier time in life. Some of my tools that I brought along had been in a back corner for a while and had a collection of dust. I had to stir things up to retrieve them and put them to use again. I found that those tools were just as useful now as they were the day I first used them. God is saying today to stir up those things that brought blessings to the kingdom of God in the past. They are still useful and usable tools in the kingdom today. You may have to dig them out of a dark and dusty corner, but it will feel good to use them once again. Now where did I leave my level?

July 25

Cycles

Acts 3:19–21

I work in the business of agriculture, and the segment that I am involved in is cyclical in nature. Supply and demand are the main driving forces for the crop I represent, and rainfall, drought, heat, and cold all impact results. After several years of positive influences, the negative influences hit our industry hard last year. Agriculture farm gate prices are at significant low points, and the outlook near term is bleak. I have lived long enough and have been in this industry long enough to know to enjoy the good times and the good years and to endure the less-than-desirable times.

There is a brighter day coming. In our walk with the Lord, there are times of refreshing that lift us up, and we bask in the goodness of God. At other times, we are encumbered with the load of life, and while still in the presence of God, we feel the weight of the load. Sometimes it is the walk of endurance that we must travel. Walk steadily, walk straight forward, and walk toward a brighter day. Do the things you know to do with renewed energy and zeal. Keep the faith and sustain yourself with the goodness of God that was yours in the past. Remember that God is walking with you through this difficult time, and there is a brighter day ahead. And yes, it may be on the other side of this life, but our short time here on earth pales in comparison to eternity with God. Eternity—that's forever.

July 26

Scattered

Acts 8:1–4

Yesterday, in "Today's SOAP [a daily devotional] from Pastor Leon," Brother Hiebert shared the parable of the sower who scattered seed. Today, my reading talks about the time of Jesus and the disciples as they participated in the Passover meal, just before Jesus's arrest, torture, and crucifixion. Jesus told the disciples that His arrest would cause them to scatter like lost sheep. The word *scatter* is intriguing to me because of its application in both incidents. In both occasions, something was going to take place, but there was no precision to it. The sower scattered good seed on good soil, poor soil, rocks, and hard paths. Today, when farmers plant seed, they do so with technology that accurately places the seed with precision, exactly where it is desired to be sown. With this technology, scattering seems to be a waste of time.

We do not know where all the eleven disciples scattered, but we know that they did indeed scatter. But we also know that they gathered together again several times in the next fifty days, and after the Holy Spirit fell on them, they scattered to preach the gospel throughout the known world.

Don't be surprised if it seems like God is not placing you with precision in the work of the kingdom of God. Sometimes He uses the technique of scattering to further the gospel. Today, we say it like this: Grow and excel where you are planted.

Praying It Forward

Romans 4:1–25

"Paying it ahead" is a popular social feel-good activity that is sweeping the country. Paying for the drive-through meal for the car behind you, paying for the cup of coffee and roll for the next in line. Paying for a basket full of groceries of the family next in line. All of these are worthy activities and make us feel good about ourselves. I'd like to suggest something for those of us who serve God not with just our lips but our lives as well. How about *praying* it forward? I receive many prayer requests over social media; they need the hand of God to intervene, and those requests are met with positive responses from many who say they will pray—and that is powerful.

What if we were to pray a blessing over those who did not express a need for the day or who didn't share the circumstances they found themselves in? Perhaps we have received a blessing and are basking in what God did for us. Maybe we could pray a similar blessing on someone we know or don't know.

God's Word tells us that God has an abundance of blessings that the earth and its inhabitants can't contain, and He is just waiting to pour out those blessings. Why wait until someone is in need before we pray? Let's pray blessings upon them before they have need. Pray it forward.

July 28

A Learning Experience: Leave Failure Behind

Philippians 3:13–14

If only I had known then what I know now. This is a thought that most of us think from time to time. And while we learn from our past and sometimes wish we could go back and change some things, it is impossible to do so. But we can take what we have learned and apply it to our lives today. Living a life of regret has no future except living in painful failure. Taking those lessons and applying them to life today is every bit about today's success.

The apostle Peter could have lived the rest of his life in regret that he had denied Jesus three times in the early morning of Jesus's arrest, but he chose instead to take that lesson, learn from it, and move forward with the calling God had placed on his life. Do not live in regret. Find the forgiveness that Jesus offers, step out of that controlling failure, and walk into what God has for you today. You will never regret leaving failure and regret behind and living in the fullness of life that Jesus offers.

July 29

Activity Report

Psalm 45:1

Our county fair and rodeo signal the end of summer vacation is approaching for the school kids. During the fun and activity are two days of school enrollment. And school starts in just a little over two weeks. Where did the summer go? It flew by extremely fast this year (again). I remember my schooldays, coming back to school and being asked to write about my summer vacation. I think that at times, God would like us to report on our past activities. Not that He doesn't know; rather, He wants is to reflect on what happened during this period. If I were to write such a report for my summer, it would include the Woodston Family Camp with grandkids, family vacation at the lake, selection of our new pastor, grilling out and smoking meat in the smoker, work travel and meetings, and a whole lot more. But what God really wants to know is how all the activity glorified Him and edified His church. (Whoa, now. I thought summer vacation was all about me and my activities.)

As I live my life, I come to understand, more and more, the importance of God's being a part of everything I do—even summer vacation. There a little bit of summer left. Make it count for God.

July 30

God, What Are You Doing?

Proverbs 16:9

What are you up to, God? I know that my steps are ordained of God and that He is leading the way. He doesn't care that I have more years behind me than I have ahead of me, or that my stamina doesn't match my want and ambition.

Being in the right place at the right time is something only God could orchestrate. I had a little extra time between appointments yesterday, so I pulled into a hotel and worked on emails in the then-quiet breakfast area. That's when a phone call came from a friend who just simply needed to talk to me and pray with me. I could have been driving, or in a noisy café, or doing something else, but God had led me to a quiet place, where I could spend the time needed without interruption. Why me, and why now? Those are questions to which I will find the answers as I walk this path laid out for me. Putting on my shoes of righteousness—God's righteousness, not mine.

July 31

Because

1 John 4:15–21

Because. It's a commonly used word in our culture and found in God's Word, occurring 1,138 times in the King James Version. In our conversations today, *because* will be used multiple times to express reasoning for something happening. My phone did not charge "because" I forgot to plug it in last night. In God's Word, we get many vivid pictures of what God did as God responds to the actions of people. In many cases, God responded with favor and blessing as people followed God's commands and were obedient to Him. In many other cases, God responded with anger and correction because of sin and willingness to ignore God and follow after other gods.

God still today responds to us here on earth *because*. The applications are many, and God's response is always righteous and correct. Our God is one who responds. He responds to our obedience, and He also responds to our disobedience. God's blessing and favor come from obedience.

August 1

Go for the Win

1 Corinthians 9:24

The abundance of 4-H and Open Class projects is evident at our local county fair. There is plenty of excitement, and there is also some disappointment, as projects are examined, scrutinized, and rated. Only one project in the category gets the grand-champion ribbon.

My granddaughter and grandson entered two bucket calves at the fair. After hours of work, bottle-feeding, providing water, feeding twice a day, halter breaking the calf to lead, giving baths, and combing fur, the two calves were shown to the judge and crowd that had gathered. My two grandkids showed clear excitement and anticipation.

I am proud of what they accomplished. Our granddaughter got a purple ribbon in a 4-H project, and our grandson got grand prize in Open Division. They worked hard, and their efforts showed. Our older granddaughter got purple and blue ribbons on her entries in photography, and with her very tasty entries in cooking, she got blue and red ribbons. Our younger granddaughter got a blue ribbon for entry in the style show and a purple for her food project. We are proud of their accomplishments and the learning experience they gained by being involved.

Paul, in his teaching in the New Testament, advises each of us to press on for the prize that is before us. What a parallel and lesson from real life.

#proudgrandma&grandpa

August 2

The Harvest Is Ready

John 4:35

So much to do and so little time to do it. That's life. The application for the things of God is the same. Jesus tells us to look up on the fields, as they are white unto the harvest. He also tells us that we are to pray for enough laborers to go out and reap the full harvest. So much has happened to get us to the place of harvest. Fields have been prepared, nutrients applied, and seed bought and then planted. Rain or irrigation has nourished the crop, and weeds and pests have been controlled. After allowing time for the crop to mature, now is the harvest. It is the focal point of all that has taken place prior to it. The hours, days, weeks, and months now focus on a short time called harvest. Extra workers and equipment are needed to gather the crop quickly.

The kingdom of God has similarities. There is so little time, yet so much to do. One individual cannot do it all. But with the help of the Lord, each individual can make a major contribution to the work of the kingdom of God.

If I do my part, and you do your part, much will be accomplished for the kingdom. Let's work together. It's harvest time!

August 3

It's Harvest Time

Ecclesiastes 3:1–2

Gods Word shares with us that there are proper times to sow and harvest. It's August and it's canning, pickling, and preserving time for gardeners in our part of the world. For many weeks, gardens have been planted, weeded, fertilized, watered, and cared for so that garden-fresh fruits and vegetables can be enjoyed, and overproduction can be put on the shelf or placed in the freezer to enjoy during the winter months.

It is a similar pattern for the work in the kingdom of God. I have observed many whose responsibility was to sow, feed, water, and nourish while waiting for the harvest, only to have God take them to another city and start the process all over, while another minister comes behind to collect the harvest. While both efforts are important, without the sowing and the care poured into the work, there would be no harvest of souls.

Harvest is a quick process, but it took a lot of work to bring it to that stage. My admiration swells for those who persevere in the physical tasks of sowing, feeding, and nurturing in God's vineyard, preparing for the harvest. God assures us that those efforts don't go unnoticed and will be rewarded by God Himself. I can hear God saying to the sower and the caretaker, "Well done, thou good and faithful servant. Great is thy reward."

August 4

A Proper Time

Ecclesiastes 3:1–8

Today, my travels take me far and wide across the Plains of the United States. I have been doing this job for nearly thirty years, and I still enjoy the travel, most of it driving. I love to see the progress of the crops and condition of the cattle as they graze. Recent rainfall has helped crops and pasture alike. I love harvest time, both summer and fall seasons, but a lot happens to get to a harvest time. There is preparation of the soil, needed rainfall to build the moisture profile, nutrients added to give the crop full potential, sowing of the seed and proper management to control pests and disease. Then harvest occurs when the crop is mature, and the crop is stored for future use.

Our walk with God and His moving among us has a similar process. Proper preparation of our lives must occur, much like tilling soil that hasn't seen the light of day for a long time. New ground becomes ready to generate a new crop. We must have the rain of the Holy Spirit that builds the spiritual profile of our lives, which will give the coming crop all it needs to thrive. Then the seed is sown.

The Word of God—written, proclaimed, expounded, and taught—falls into prepared and fertile soil and is ready to germinate quickly and develop into a successful crop. Continuation of the study of God's Word and surrounding ourselves with other believers helps to strengthen and encourage us as we daily live our lives before the Lord our God. Doing so keeps the "pests" at bay.

And then the harvest. I sense that a great harvest of souls is at hand. All the preparatory work has occurred. We are now at the door of harvest. As I look out over this sea of humanity, I see a bumper crop. It's harvest time—thirty-, sixty-, even one-hundredfold. Just for giggles and grins, take your church attendance and multiply it by thirty, sixty, or even one hundred. That's God's promise. I am amazed!

August 5

I Am Part of the Plan

Jeremiah 29:11

The camper is stuffed full of Grandma, Grandpa, parents, and grandkids. Pretty sure that somebody snuck their pet fish in here too. We are camped at a lake, and play, fishing, biking, and much more—even s'mores—await us. All this activity is because LaDonna and I fell in love and married, and forty-six years, three children, and seven grandchildren later, here we are. Human life is meant, in part, for procreation, and I told LaDonna this morning that all of this going on this week is because of us. When I consider our part in the plan of God, I realize that God, the master planner, has a lot going on. I'm thankful that we get to be a part of His plan. I'm thankful for our time together this week—just a small part of God's great-big plan. I hope He has some great-big fish as a part of His plan for us this week.

August 6

Disciple Selection

Mark 1:17

Yesterday was a day of fishing. We all caught at least one fish and most caught several. It was exciting enough to want to go again today. I think it's interesting that four of the five known occupations of the disciples were described as "fisherman."

It would be reasonable to think that prior to selecting the disciples, Jesus had observed these men in their work and their environment. I also think that Jesus selected these men not because of their ability but because of their potential.

Lord, look down on us and choose us for our potential, not just our abilities. Yesterday we caught small fish, with a couple of nice ones. Today, we go after bigger fish. Yesterday, our abilities limited us in your kingdom, O God. Today, use us to the potential You see in us.

August 7

Storms Come and Go

Psalm 107:29

A camping trip in the Plains area of the United States is not complete without a good thunderstorm. Fortunately, it waited until we were up this morning. Not sure that having five grandkids jump into our bed would have been termed "fun." But storms come and then they go. Later we will swim, fish, cook out, and have s'mores.

Life offers its own series of storms. Some are short-lived and some last awhile, but they all move on at some time. Life goes on, and we pick up where we left off.

Weather the storm. There is sunshine on the other side, and with God as your strength, you will make it through every storm.

August 8

Keep the Rod Tip Up

John 16:12–16

We have fished the last two evenings and have caught a lot of little fish and a couple of bigger fish, which has encouraged bragging rights for a couple of our group. Grandpa's job is to fix fishing poles, bait hooks, remove fish, untangle lines, and tell the grandkids, "Keep the rod tip up."

At times I have some understanding that what I write here is a lot like encouraging you to keep the rod tip up. In fishing, you want to keep the tip of the rod up so that the line and rod, working together, can better control the fish that is on the hook. Doing this allows the fisherman to feel what the fish is doing and how much energy the fish has. It also gives the fisherman more control over the fish to wear it out and bring it to the shore.

I love being sensitive to the things of God. Today I am keeping my rod tip up. I encourage you to do the same. Fish on!

August 9

Protected

Psalm 18:1–3

Our campsite is located below the dam of a large lake. The park includes a swimming beach and a fishing lake. Hidden from our view is the large lake above the dam. This great berm of rolled earth and rock separates us and keeps about a hundred-foot depth of water covering several thousand acres from washing us away. I am thankful that the dam is there and for the park we enjoy because of it.

Sometimes in living life, God, our protector, has built a "dam" that separates us from harm. We feel the same heat on both sides and experience similar rainfall, but the dam keeps us safe. I may not see everything that is on the other side of this dam, but I can clearly see the dam from where I am. I am thankful for God's protection. His protection will never fail.

August 10

Thrive

Philippians 4:11

The past few days of summer have seen very hot (95–100 degrees) and very windy weather on the Plains. Lawns, gardens, pastures, and field crops are showing the influence of this harsh weather. But as I look at the overall situation, I see several species of plants that have adapted to this harsh change of climate. Those plants do not appear to suffer and even seem to thrive when other types of foliage nearby just give up.

In life, the climate is ever-changing. God gives His people resiliency to adapt. The situation we find ourselves in may not be the most desirable, but our Lord God Almighty, who rules from heaven, helps us.

Be a resilient Christ-follower today. Let God equip you to be the person you should be in this harsh climate. By the grace of God, you will thrive.

August 11

Forced Changes

1 Corinthians 7:29–31

Sometimes urgency forces us to make a change in plans—like a hurricane sweeping into Texas from the warm Gulf waters. I'm sure many plans were canceled because of this storm. Sometimes God places urgency into our lives to force change. How many times have I been forced to change but only with kicking and screaming (at least figuratively)? I have found that when God places urgency in my life, it is for a valid reason.

Lord God, help me to see that what is being revealed to me is just part of a greater overall plan that you have for my life.

You may feel urgency in your life as well, something that you have continually put off for quite some time. Don't ignore the urgency God is placing in your life. Act on it now, rather than later. God has a greater plan in store for you—change. But God-change is always a better thing than what I have today.

Like a Mighty Sea

Jeremiah 31:35

A fast-moving category-3 hurricane is enough to deal with, but when that same storm type slows down, the winds last longer, and the rainfall is measured in feet and not inches. Destruction and flooding are horrific, and loss of life occurs.

Great devastation occurs as nature battles against itself and humans and their things. While it is easy to view what is happening to Texas and to the millions in the path of this huge storm as nothing but devastation, I believe that we can draw a spiritual parallel from it.

The hymn writer Henry Zelley penned these words:

Like a mighty sea, like a mighty sea,
Comes the Love of Jesus sweeping over me!
The waves of Glory roll, the Savior to extol,
Comes the Love of Jesus sweeping o'er my soul!

I see in my spirit the Holy Spirit of God sweeping into America as a great, overwhelming presence, much like how the present hurricane is presenting itself. I see evil being uprooted and swept away as men, women, young people, and children are forever changed by the saving power of Jesus Christ. I see the power of God falling and flowing in unprecedented amounts—amounts never before attained. I see a nation humbled in the presence of almighty God as He displays His power and authority, and His people rightly display the power and authority granted to them through Jesus Christ.

I grew up in an area of the country that would experience long-term droughts. When rains finally came, we would go outside and stand in the rain, rejoicing in what God was sending our way. Lord God Almighty, I am standing here expectantly, waiting for the rain of Your Spirit. Is that the sound of abundance of rain that I hear? I think it is.

August 13

Help Is on the Way

Hebrews 13:16

I was driving a main north/south highway in the Texas Panhandle yesterday. I saw the goodness of America traveling alongside of me as I noticed several convoys of men and women in pickups with work shells—some pulling trailers, van trucks, and other vehicles heading south, presumably headed to the hurricane-impacted area of Texas. Many of those traveling were from several states away and had left jobs, home, and family to lend a hand, doing whatever they could to help those in need. I do not know how long these helpers will stay. I only know that they are desiring to help. Can I say it like this? The storm is not driving folks out of Texas; rather, it is bringing them in by the thousands.

True American spirit is showing up in waves of convoys coming to help those in need. That's the America that needs to be portrayed on all media outlets. Please do not refer to me as a person of political affiliation anymore. Please, just call me an American. May that be said about the tens of thousands who are coming into a devastated area to help. May it be said of those who have donated what they can to help in this time of need. We are Americans.

August 14

The Power of Nature

Psalm 95:3–5

Though the devastation that has occurred in southeast Texas is mind-boggling, even more so is the power of God expressed in this natural disaster. For instance, the amount of rain that fell in Houston and the surrounding area during Hurricane Harvey is estimated to have been 61.3 million acre feet. To put that into perspective, my home state, Kansas, is roughly two hundred miles wide by four hundred miles long and contains 52.66 million acres. There was enough rainfall in Harvey that fell in the Houston area to have blanketed the state of Kansas with over fourteen inches of rain, enough to have caused severe flooding over the entire state.

The ability of Creator God to move that much water volume from the Gulf of Mexico to the Houston area in just a few short hours is unfathomable to the human mind. Whether God sent the storm or whether He allowed it to happen is debatable, but in any case, we must be amazed at the power that was contained in this storm called Harvey. Yes, even in a natural disaster such as Harvey, we have only to take a moment and observe the power of God and realize that we can join with the prophet of old and ask this question: "What is man, that thou art mindful of him?" (Psalm 8: 4) Yes, absolutely, He is big enough to rule the mighty universe, yet small enough to live within my heart. My God is truly amazing, and He is *really. really big*!

August 15

Life-Controlling Issues: Let Faith Be in Control

Romans 10:17

We all face life-controlling issues—and there are many. It may be addiction to drugs, alcohol, sex, tobacco, food, soda, porn, even shoes and clothes, just to name a few. These seemingly insignificant things, initially, can turn into monster life-controlling issues. God's Word says that we, as Christians, can take authority over these things with the Word of God. God's Word teaches that faith comes from hearing, and hearing comes from the Word of God. When you force yourself to replace the life-controlling substances with the Word of

God—and yes, you can force yourself—you will find that the Word of God will build your faith, give you resistance to those controlling desires, and satisfy your every need.

I suggest that when you find yourself in want of more of your life-controlling junk that instead of lighting that cigarette, or opening the fridge, or nursing that bottle, or viewing that porn, or whatever is controlling you, you open God's Word and read until His Word has replaced that craving. God's Word brings satisfaction—complete and whole.

Just open God's Word when those pangs hit you. And yes, it will be multiple times a day. And stay in God's Word until it satisfies your need. The key to this simple process is replacing your life-controlling addiction with the Word of God. Simple, but force yourself to pick up the Word of God first and read until it has satisfied your craving. God can and will do this for you.

August 16

The Sanctuary of the Home

Psalm 17:6–9

It is appalling that the very place that is prepared to be a sanctuary and a place of safety—the home—has now become, in many cases, a place of abuse, molestation, incest, and rape. I'm not referencing any one circumstance, but I know there are significant happenings of such and increasing reports of this sickening sin. Predators living in the home or who are invited into the home take advantage of innocence and opportunity. We used to look at third-world countries and excuse this behavior because the culture didn't know better, but this culture of sin is invading our elite society like a plague.

Almighty God, we need a revelation of the sin that so easily besets us, a conviction of that sin that causes repentance, and a complete turning away from sin. Almighty God, we are a sinful people in need of repentance and a true turning away from sin. Jesus, I pray for those who cannot protect themselves and who are vulnerable to such sinful behavior. Guard them with Your mighty right hand, in Jesus's name.

August 17

Anticipation

Romans 8:18–25

It seems that all of nature is anticipating what I will call "last days." We are experiencing September-like weather here in mid-August, and while that's not unusual for a day or two, two weeks is totally unusual. There have been earthquakes in unusual places, like the Central Plains of the USA. Signs and wonders have occurred in the heavens—and more. We, as the bride of Christ, should also greatly anticipate the soon-appearing bridegroom, Jesus Christ, in the clouds to call us home to be with him eternally.

Just as an engaged woman long anticipates and grows more excited each day as her wedding day approaches, we, as Christians, ought to be in *great anticipation* of that day. If your "exciter" is not working right, then I encourage you to have some maintenance done. Attend a church that teaches and preaches on the Second Coming and the "catching away" of the church.

Let excitement build in me and you, just as it seems that God's nature is building excitement within itself. I'm anticipating the call any moment now, and I am excited!

August 18

Exceeding Joy

Psalm 96:11–13

Surprises occur often in life, and many of these experiences are pleasant, even joyous. God has made the human spirit capable of being overcome by the experience of a pleasant surprise. Sure, other surprises occur that are not pleasant, but be sure to enjoy those that are, even the small ones. God weaves His presence into the fabric of our lives, and in the weaving process, He unveils pleasant surprises. Don't overlook these little gems that occur throughout life. Let them grasp your spirit and lift you up. God has a pleasant surprise in store for you today. It may be small, but it's there for you to experience.

August 19

Love and Show It

1 John 4:7

The showing of affection is an important part of our emotional makeup. If we pen up affection and don't let it exhibit itself, it turns to bitterness. We learn in scripture that God first loved us. His love and affection toward us, despite our sinfulness, was full and complete. There was no bitterness. The world around us needs the affection that each of us has available to us.

I have observed those who have shown no affection and the bitterness that has become their lives. I have discovered the following about showing affection: I may not get any return affection from the one to whom I show affection, but my spirit thrives because I have done so. Often, the affection is returned many times over. How much I would have missed, had I not shown affection first.

Give affection. When you do it, will be returned to you full, pressed down, and spilling over.

August 20

New Every Day

Lamentations 3:22–23

I love new. There is nothing like experiencing something new—something that is refreshing and delightful. For parents, treating your baby to the new taste of ice cream reflects what *new* means. The word *new* occurs 496 times in the New Living Translation of God's Word and 136 times in the King James Version. God's Word speaks of new life when we receive Jesus as Savior. Old things have passed away, and behold, all things become new. Once that baby has ice cream, you will never get away with just having ice cream for yourself any longer. The baby delights in the newfound taste and experience.

God tells us that His mercies are new every morning. Yesterday's mercies are obsolete. Today's are brand new. It's like getting to drive a brand-new car or truck. It's got a new smell, a new look, a new feel. That's a Christian's life today. It's brand-spanking new. Enjoy this new day and God's new mercies. It's refreshing, like ice cream for the soul!

August 21

A Dry and Thirsty Land

Psalm 63:1–11

Soft, slow, gentle, and satisfying—these four words I am ascribing to the rainfall over the last several hours. Our soil was parched and needed refreshing rainfall, and God gave what was needed, with more rainfall promised in the next several days. Throughout God's Word, we discover writers who were going through dry or drought periods in their lives, and they voiced their concerns to the one who not only heard but answered their prayers. I sense in my spirit that we are entering a new season where the Spirit of God will fall on a dry and thirsty people. They will absorb all that God pours out and will respond to this new outpouring in power and faith, seizing the opportunity to do so. As the rain has fallen, the grass and perennial plants have quickly responded with greening up and growth. Lord God Almighty, may I respond in a similar manner as Your Holy Spirit flows through me.

August 22

Living a Full Life

Acts 2:28

There is a distinct difference in living your life to the fullest and living a full life. Our culture fills our time every moment of every day. It's not unusual to wake up to chores left from yesterday, with added chores and tasks that can't be finished today—and the cycle continues. Being totally consumed by life's activity is not the same as a living a full life.

The enemy of our souls would have us ensnared in such an active life that we don't have time for important things—things like standing still in the quiet of dawn and letting the gentleness of the transition of night to day soothe our souls; things like darkness fading to light as we watch; the air filled with birds starting their day with singing as they stay perched in their nightly resting area; soft breezes bringing the smell of flowers, cedar wood, and moisture-laden air to our senses. And there is time to listen to God (1 Samuel 3:9–10).

The creation of humans was, in part, a desire of God to be able to communicate with humans on a personal basis—to ask how you are, what your plans are, what your needs are—and to share with you His plans, His needs, and His presence. Time spent with God—now that's a full life.

August 23

Live in the Light

John 8:12

Blindness must be a terrifying experience. It's an experience I cannot understand because I can see. Although I have been in the dark many times, I am certainly partial to having enough light to at least see my way around.

God desires that we live in the light (John 8:12). Throughout God's Word, we find that the three persons of God—the Father, Son, and Holy Spirit—quickly bring light to everything. On the first day of creation, God made light.

Why is our world living in a strong desire for darkness? Because the enemy of our souls desires to keep us from the light of God. There are many places in our world where God's light needs to shine. One prominent place is in our government.

Lord God, I join others, including the Reverend Franklin Graham, in praying that the light of God's Word would be turned on in our government and that spiritual darkness would be scattered by the light of Your Word. Let us not be a blind people being led by the blind, but let us awaken to the light that You desire to shine upon us and through us. Oh Lord, let your light shine brilliantly through us as we are led by You today.

August 24

Little Things Matter

1 Corinthians 12:12

Little things matter. Sometimes, they matter a lot.

On the older John Deere tractors, the drawbar was attached to the tractor by a single steel pin. This pin could be taken out and the drawbar easily removed. On occasion, the pin would work itself out on its own while pulling equipment in the field, causing the piece of equipment to detach from the tractor, unplugging the hydraulics and anything else attached. You would be going through the field with equipment working as it should, when suddenly the tractor would lurch as the pin came out and the equipment became detached. You would look back and see the equipment stopped in the field, with the drawbar of the tractor laying on the ground, and the equipment still attached. The small drawbar pin that attached the drawbar to the tractor was the only piece that made everything else work as it was supposed to. It was hidden from sight and out of the way, yet it was a small part that was vital to the operation of the tractor and equipment.

Our Christian walk has similar applications. Small things play important roles in building the kingdom of God (1 Corinthians 12:12). Perhaps you view what God has you involved in as small or insignificant, but God has a divine purpose and plan for that small, insignificant part to be a vital part of building His kingdom. Yes, friend, little things matter.

August 25

Forgiven and Forgotten

Hebrews 8:11–13

You may have spent the last several days beating up on yourself for actions that were wrong, actions that not only impacted you but many around you. A vivid realization—that you can apologize for what has been done but you can't undo it—may have gripped your life, becoming the controlling factor of your life since it happened. Regret and remorse have filled your thoughts, and you can't stop thinking about what could have been, had you taken different actions.

I am here to tell you that the best and most complete restoration process known to humankind is confession to God through our Savior Jesus Christ, who has the power to not only forgive but to immediately forget and never remember it again. You may ask, "How in the world can my actions, which are known to so many, ever be forgotten?" Unfortunately, people will retain the memory, but God's promise is that when we confess and ask forgiveness, He does forgive, and the action of sin is buried in the deep sea of His forgetfulness. That's God's promise. And His promise counts the most.

There are penalties for our wrong actions, but to know that God forgives and then forgets—now, that's something that you can experience today. That's part of the reason Jesus returned to Jerusalem on Palm Sunday so many years ago. He knew that death on a cross awaited Him, but He also knew that you and I would need the forgiveness of sin that the giving of His life's blood would bring. He did it for you. No matter the wrong that you've done, He did it for you.

God Makes a Way of Escape

1 Corinthians 10:13

It was problematic from the very beginning. God gave to humans a will that they could control, but He also allowed for powerful temptation to entice and lure humans into sinful activity. It all started in the garden of Eden with the first man and woman that God created. If any humans had the perfect characteristics that God intended for humans to have, Adam and Eve had them. They were God's intended creation.

Since the fall of man, the problem with the will of humans and the enticing lure of sin has been handed down to every generation. The temptation and lure of sin will happen, and the enemy of our souls will sometimes bombard us with so much activity that it seems overwhelming. How do we overcome the onslaught of the enemy, especially when it seems that he has backed us into a corner with no way of escape? God's promise to us, through His Word, is that He will not allow any temptation into our life that we cannot overcome or find a way of escape (1 Corinthians 10:13).

It may seem like we are backed into a corner, but we serve a God who is more than capable of making a way of escape. He can make a door where there isn't one. The problem with you and me is that we don't look for the way of escape.

The Israelites were pinned between the great Egyptian army and the Red Sea. They were tempted to give in to the enemy and return to Egypt and their lives of slavery. There was no way of escape—or so it seemed. God opened a door completely impossible to humans. He miraculously opened the Red Sea and provided a dry path for their escape (Exodus 14:1–31).

Has enticement and the lure of sin so captivated your life that it seems hopeless? I declare to you that God can and will provide a way out with His miraculous power and might. How do you overcome the onslaught of enticement and the lure of sin? Stand firm in the God of your salvation, Jesus Christ, until He provides a way of escape. Yes, there may be some tough times and circumstances, but *He will make a way.*

August 27

Wars and Rumors of Wars

Matthew 24:6

Wars and rumors of wars are prevailing elements of our day. God's Word declares that this is one of the major signs of the nearness of Jesus's return.

The Korean War was fought in the years of 1950–1953, and now, some sixty-five years later, it appears that a second Korean conflict is escalating. The Middle East remains a hot spot of conflict, as Christianity is the focus of complete annihilation, first by Satan and then by those who are his followers. Britain exits the European Union, and internal turmoil ensues. The United States' election divides a nation, and there is unrest around the world. Clearly, we are living in the end times, as stated throughout God's Word.

What is our focus to be during these days? Certainly, if we observe any news source, we will be bombarded with what is occurring, but our focus must be on the one who is waiting in the throne room of heaven for God the Father to say, "Now!" Our focus must be on making sure our families are prepared to join the celebration of the marriage supper of the Lamb in heaven and not be left here on earth to endure the hardship left for humankind, or eternal damnation. Our focus must be on sharing the good news with every person here on earth.

Get ready. A shaking is coming that will crumble life on earth, as we know it. There is coming a "reaching out to God," as never before seen in the history of our world. Previous world revivals will pale in comparison. I can't wait to watch it unfold, either here personally or observing it from my eternal home in heaven. Even so, come, Lord Jesus.

August 28

Priest, Temple Worker, or Good Samaritan

Luke 10:29–37

It's a fact that in our culture, one can be backed into a corner, where there's an army of opportunistic human vultures who will be ready to join in a feeding frenzy to devour body, mind, soul, and spirit.

I have watched as vultures in the wild fly high above the earth, looking for a carcass or a dying animal that they can swarm in on. It begins with one bird landing near the carcass or weak animal, testing the situation. If there is little or no life, then other vultures join in, surrounding the animal. I have seen several dozen vultures surround animals as they breathe their last breaths. Once the vultures determine that the animal is indeed dead or weak, they will attack it on its back side. When the animal quits offering any defense moves, the vultures swoop in and begin a feeding frenzy.

Our human culture and human nature are to act like vultures. But God has put a new nature in our hearts and lives when we become Christians. We now help the weak, the fallen, the oppressed, the helpless, the blind, and the hungry. We come along and bind up their wounds and take them to a place of safety (Luke 10:29–37). Those who are vulnerable are all around us.

Lord God Almighty, don't let me just casually glance their way. Help me to stop what I am doing and help them along their way. And when I do, I know it will help me more than the help I offer. God's Word declares that in our giving, it will be returned, pressed down, shaken together, and running over.

I love a running-over life.

August 29

No Needs in Heaven

Revelation 21:1–7

Sometimes I reach out to God in my deepest need, and it is important that I do. At other times, when my needs aren't so pressing, I reach out to God in worship and praise, both of which are equally important.

Many times, the circumstances of life drive us to pray to the living God who hears us and answers our prayers. At other times, God desires to hear our worship and praise to Him, God Almighty, who alone is worthy of our worship and praise. Each prayer, whether out of need or out of praise, is heard by God and has His attention.

A scene is described about heaven that catches my attention. Heaven is a place where there will be no need on our part—no circumstances of life for which we will need God's help. Rather, all those in heaven will be gathered around the throne of God, praising Him, saying, "Holy, holy, holy." If I will be participating in this worship in heaven, I can do it on earth as well (Revelation 5:13).

Father God Almighty, the Son of God, Jesus Christ, and the Comforter, the Holy Spirit of God, are worthy to be praised.

August 30

The Heart of the Matter

Philippians 2:1–11

We often hear the phrase, "the heart of the matter." It speaks of dismantling the insignificant veneer or facade and getting a look at the true matter. There is no question that our world is at unrest today. That unrest is just a facade covering the real matter that burns in the hearts of individuals. The heart of the matter is this: separation from God creates unrest. Violence will not settle the unrest. Things will not satisfy the unrest. Political power will not cure the unrest. Only Jesus can remove the unrest and bring peace into a life.

Lord God Almighty, as the unrest of this world swirls around me, may I find peace in the shelter of Your arms. And may the eyes of those who experience unrest be opened to reveal the heart of the matter.

August 31

Request or Praise

Philippians 4:6

Today, I had a long list of needs as I came before the Lord God Almighty. Bringing needs before the Lord God—and sometimes long lists—is not unusual for the children of God. We are encouraged to do so with faith that God will intervene in our affairs and grant our requests.

God's Word tells us that we are to make our requests known to our Lord God, and we do so by lifting them up in prayer before God the Father.

Today, this realization came to me, as I knew that my list was lengthy and would take up quite a bit of my quiet time with God. God already knew everything—absolutely everything—that I was going to bring to Him. Nothing was going to catch Him unaware. God knew what I wanted. Did I know what God wanted? He desired my praise to Him. I could simply say to Him, "God Almighty, You know all my requests and even the ones that aren't on the list. You knew even before I did that they would be there today."

So instead of going through my list, which God already knew, I took time to praise God for His love, mercy, kindness, and tenderheartedness.

God does inhabit the praise of His people. I can rejoice today, knowing that God cares about my needs, but I can also rejoice in knowing that He is present as I praise Him.

September 1

God-Given Dominion

Genesis 1:26–29

In Genesis 1, the first thing God did after He created man was to give man dominion over all His creation (Genesis 1:26–29). God's last creation, man, would have authority over every other creation. Included was all the fish, plants, birds, livestock, and every living organism. God gave to man a tremendous authority when He gave him the directive to have dominion over all other creation.

That authority was not revoked when God removed Adam and Eve from the garden of Eden. That powerful authority is still in effect today. But what does that mean for our world?

When we view authority in the setting of the first man, we think about domesticating cows, horses, dogs, and cats; growing vegetables, orchards, and vines in an orderly fashion; removing weeds; and picking hungry insects off the tended plants. In today's culture and with the wonderful beneficial technology that is available to us, having dominion over all of God's creation now includes modern medicine (many of us take a medication that was not available one hundred years ago), modern transportation, modern communication, and modern housing. Almost everything that we have today is because man was given dominion over all those other things. He took that authority and created these modern conveniences.

Did I mention herbs and plants? I work for a company that has wisely invested a great number of resources in exercising dominion and authority over plant life. Our scientists and research workers are doing exactly what God gave man authority to do with plant life. Some believe that we, as humans, should not do anything with regard to having dominion over the rest of God's creation, but I challenge that premise. If our culture is to feed a hungry world, we must take the dominion and authority God has given us and utilize it in creating safe, nutritious, productive, environmentally coexistent foods and feedstocks that will allow our culture to feed a hungry world. Any effort to try to revoke man's God-given authority to have dominion over all the rest of God's creation is an effort to challenge God's authority.

September 2

The Process of Arriving at Harvest

1 Corinthians 3:1–9

We planted a forage yield trial yesterday and plan to plant three more today. What we planted yesterday will be irrigated today and will be cared for until harvest time next May. In doing so, I can see clearly the process of the concept of some planting, some watering, and then harvest. It does not occur overnight. There are seasons of time that happen for each of these parts of the overall plan. For the test plots, the planting went very quickly, getting the entire plot done in a couple of hours. The irrigation will be ongoing through the fall and again in early spring to be sure that the plants survive and are healthy for harvest. There will be several applications of water, and some watering will occur through natural rainfall, but we still must rely on our ability to water. And then next May, it will be time to harvest.

Again, it was an operation that was done in a single day's time but will show the results of the planting and the irrigation that took place over time. I see in my spirit that we are approaching the last "irrigation" cycle for the church of Jesus Christ. It perhaps has already started. The harvest is near, and we have one last opportunity to ensure that the harvest is plentiful and great. I'm so glad to be a part of the team focused on harvest. Join me in being a planter or irrigator in the kingdom of God. It's great knowing that your contribution will increase the harvest.

September 3

Signs and Wonders

Hebrews 2:4

God's Word speaks of miracles and exploits that will occur that are beyond the thoughts or imaginations of humans.

As a boy, I was often told that I had a big imagination. I dreamed of being the Lone Ranger, Superman, Matt Dillon, Roy Rogers, and many more of my childhood heroes as I joined them in the fight against lawlessness. As I grew older, my imaginations changed, but they were still big, and many of those either came to pass or have been put to rest.

Today, when it comes to the things of God and the kingdom of God here on earth, I still have a big imagination and a huge expectation.

Lord God Almighty, I ask today that you would cause faith in my life to rise up to the expectation that you desire in me and that the power of God would be evident in manifestation of what Your Word declares is available to Your children. I start with a declaration that I am a child of God and that I am a joint heir with Jesus, as declared in Your Word. Father God, help me to live my life worthy of that family heritage.

September 4

Obey the Law

Genesis 2:15–17

Laws have been a part of culture since Adam and Eve, when God told them not to eat the fruit of two distinct trees. They could do anything else without restriction, but obviously, they could not restrain themselves from breaking God's command.

Since that time, God gave to Moses, to the children of Israel, and to us today the Ten Commandments, as well as many more. Jesus said that those Ten Commandments were summarized into two: love God, and love man.

Since then, individuals have mandated many laws to help society and to help humans live together peaceably. For the most part, laws are for our protection and for our good, and certainly, I disagree with some laws. But laws are a factor for our whole and wholesome lives here on earth.

Will there be laws in heaven? I believe so. God says that no sin will enter heaven. There will be no sorrow. Again, for our good and protection, God will have eternal laws in heaven. But I personally hope the speed limit laws go away.

September 5

Family Time

Revelation 19:5–9

I look forward to later today, when all our children will be here, along with grandkids. What an exciting time. Some of my favorite memories growing up included going to my grandparents' home for holiday family meals. We will gather around the family table this evening and enjoy each other's company for the few hours that we can all be together. We have a Father in heaven who also has a desire to spend time with His family. I believe there is anticipation in heaven regarding the marriage supper of the Lamb, but until that appointed time, God still has a desire for table fellowship with His people. Take time to spend time with God this holiday weekend around His table. He eagerly anticipates that time. I know because He made me like Him—to enjoy His family in fellowship together.

September 6

Human Attributes?

Genesis 1:26–31

We often assign human attributes to God. God can see, hear, speak, and act. But it was God who said, "Let us (Father, Son, and Holy Spirit) make man in Our own image." It is we who were given godly attributes, not the other way around.

As I think about that this morning, I am overwhelmed with the care in which Creator God made man. God made me able to see all that He created. He enabled me to hear, not just the sounds around me and other humans speaking but to hear His voice.

God gave me a voice to extol His virtues and not curse His holy name, a voice to tell others about the love of God. God gave to me the ability to think and to act on those thoughts.

It was not just a whim that God created this earth and all that is in it and then created man. His was a well-thought-out plan. And He has given me that same ability.

I will not try to bring God down to my level of understanding. God has created me to be like Him in all my human characteristics. I want to be more like Him.

September 7

Intimately Knowing the Voice of God

John 10:22–30

Many positive benefits come from having a close relationship with Jesus Christ, the Son of God. Certainly, the knowledge that I will spend eternity in heaven, in God's presence, is a key positive factor, but many more benefits are part of the package.

A lot of individuals have only a shallow relationship with the Savior, Jesus Christ. Many times, for those in a shallow relationship, recognizing the difference between the voice of God and the voice of the evil one is difficult. We know that the evil one is willing to put voices inside our minds. He is masterful in disguising himself as a good voice, all the while luring us into deep sin. Knowing the difference in voices comes from having a deep and close relationship with Jesus.

Jesus said, "My sheep hear my voice." (John 10:27) Yes, there have been times in my life when I have asked, "God, is this You speaking to me?" It was then that I listened closely. I want to know for certain that it is the voice of the Great Shepherd. Jesus assures us that He will not lead us on the wrong path or into swirling water. If we find ourselves in those situations, then we have heard the wrong voice.

Today, let's covenant to renew our close relationship with God through Jesus Christ. He is willing to speak clearly to us, and I want to be sure that I know His voice.

September 8

Seeking Out an Answer

Proverbs 25:1

The wisdom in God's Word tells us that the king delights in seeking out an answer to a matter. I am not a king, but life and my occupation sometimes bring about perplexing issues. In my occupation, when I am puzzled about something, I can call upon a wealth of knowledgeable people with vast experience levels. Most of the time they are very helpful in solving problems. Recently, I have been overwhelmed with a perplexing problem that I have shared with those who have long and extensive experience in solving such problems. So far, the response that I have received from them is, "This is perplexing." Certainly not the answer that I was hoping for.

It would be very easy to throw my hands up in the air, go to someone experiencing a problem, and say, "I don't have an answer," and go on. But I think wisdom says, "I don't have an answer today, but don't give up. I am still working on it." God's Word promises that if any man—and I am an "any man"—lacks wisdom, let him ask of God, and God will provide it in liberal amounts. I hold on to that promise today.

Lord God Almighty, I lack wisdom in this matter. Guide my steps, my thoughts, my direction, and my follow-through as I seek out the answer.

Guided to Safety

Psalm 31:3

Both of my flights yesterday were over heavy clouds. The weather below ranged from heavy snow to severe thunderstorms, to fog and drizzle, and everything in between. While above the clouds, I could see vast distances around me, but then it came time for the plane to descend to its destination. That meant flying through the clouds and trusting that the technology on board the plane was communicating properly with the technology being sent to guide us safely to our intended destination.

While flying through the clouds, visibility was extremely poor, and at times I could not even see the wing tip on my side of the plane. The descent seemed to take an extra-long time, as the cloud layer was very thick. Suddenly, the plane broke through the clouds and, less than a minute later, touched down on the runway, landing safely.

Sometimes our life seems to be clouded. We have no sense of direction, only that life is passing by very quickly. Sometimes we find that we are above the clouds, yet sense that our feet need to be on the ground. Sometimes life's foundation appears at just the last minute, and at other times, we are surrounded by the clouds of life.

The plane flew through the clouds because it was communicating with a source of technology that allowed it to do so. We can fly through the clouds of life because we trust in the one, Jesus Christ, who can give us direction and stability, even when life around us is in turmoil.

September 10

Imitation, Be the Example

1 Corinthians 11:1

I have heard it said that imitation is the greatest form of flattery. Millions of dollars have been made marketing imitation products. Imitations of valuable watches and jewelry mimic the real thing. There are even imitations of food ingredients and food items that are marketed. Most of the time, imitation is of lesser quality. But when it comes to grandchildren imitating their parents and grandparents, imitation is priceless.

My grandson desires to do everything his father does, imitating his actions, activities, demeanor, and behavior. Imitation is a powerful teacher.

Paul the apostle, in writing to the Ephesian church, tells us to imitate Christ in everything we do. Beginning with God Himself, imitation is a valued component of our lives. It is a natural instinct of human life. Even today, I catch myself imitating my earthly father. I also desire to be caught imitating my heavenly Father.

Imitation—God's plan for perfection. Only God could put it in that perspective.

September 11

9/11—Just a Glimpse of the Future

Matthew 24:1–22

Nearly everyone over the age of twenty-five will remember exactly where they were and what they were doing on that late summer morning of September 11, 2001. LaDonna and I were preparing meals for a ministers' retreat when we heard the news that a plane had flown into one of the World Trade towers in New York City. This news was followed by news of a second plane flying into the second tower, another into the Pentagon, and a third plane crashing to the ground. Our world reeled in emotions as terror ran rampant across our nation. These acts of terror brought our nation, for a brief time, to a place of looking to Almighty God in heaven for peace, direction, and help in our time of trouble.

Our nation has healed, but a large scar remains. And we have removed ourselves from that place of looking to God for help and direction because we can take care of ourselves. God had our attention on 9/11/2001. If I understand God's Word, there will be other, even larger events that will impact our world, and God will once again have our attention. My question is this: since I know that these types of events, revealed in God's Word, will take place, and ultimately God will have our attention, why keep moving in a direction away from God, thus forcing His action to regain our attention? If we, as a nation, would choose to focus on God today, give Him our attention, and chase hard after Him, then perhaps we would once again find favor from God and His hand of protection and blessing upon the United States of America.

September 12

Jesus Is Real in My Life

2 Corinthians 3

Jesus is real. Sometimes the busyness of life causes us to overlook the reality—the fact that Jesus is real; to consider that, for Christians, the Son of God lives in us. Now that is real. God Himself resides within us, not because our lives are perfect or even attractive, but because He cares enough—more than just enough—to make our lives His dwelling place.

While walking this earth in human flesh, Jesus said of Himself that He had no dwelling place. Now, after His resurrection, His dwelling place is in our lives. That is real.

God lives in me—simple, plain, broken, hard-headed, crusty ol' me. Jesus chose to do so, and I am so glad.

Jesus is real. I know because He lives in me.

September 13

Life-Giving Blood

Hebrews 9:14

We have purchased some paint for the interior of our home. It sits in the basement waiting to be applied. We have paid for it, we have it in our possession, and we even have a plan for it. All we lack is the application. Application requires extra effort.

In order for anyone to spend eternity with God the Father, God the Son, and God the Holy Spirit, the blood of Jesus Christ must be applied to his or her life through God's salvation. Our salvation was bought and paid for by Jesus's death on the cross. There was a plan in place when Jesus went to the cross, and that plan—that work—is finished. All that needs to happen now is for it to be applied.

You may never have had the blood of Jesus applied to your life. Everything is ready. Today is the day to decide to make the application. Let Jesus put a brand-new "you" on display for all the world to see. Ask Jesus to apply His blood to your life, and ask Him to forgive all your sin. Ask Him for His wonderful salvation. It has been bought and paid for.

September 14

My Own Chains

Colossians 4:18

The apostle Paul, writing to the Colossians, ends his epistle with these words: "Here is my greeting in my own handwriting—Paul. Remember my chains. May God's grace be with you" (Colossians 4:18 NLT).

"Remember my chains." Of all the things that he wanted to convey to the church, in his own handwriting, he writes, "Remember my chains." There are a lot of things we might remember about the apostle Paul and his ministry, but here, he simply asked us to remember him as he was held as a prisoner in chains.

Today, Christians in many parts of our world are in chains because of their belief in Jesus Christ. Many are slaughtered for their faith. Today, I reflect on Paul's chains, though I am confident that he is now in the presence of Jesus. Today, I choose to remember those who are, at this moment, in chains because of their faith in Jesus Christ. If I were one of them, I believe that I would also want you to remember my chains.

September 15

Whatever It Takes

Psalm 77:16–20

As we watch yet another major hurricane take aim at the USA, our inclination is to call upon God to steer it in a different direction or to calm the storm, and I believe those are legitimate requests of God. I sincerely do ask God to protect lives and property that lies in the path of the storm. Long before the hurricanes formed in the Atlantic and Gulf areas, people of God were praying to a holy and righteous God that He would send revival to America and that God would do "whatever it takes" to bring America back to God.

Many prophetic messages in the last couple of years share the promise that this nation and our world will be shaken as never before, and perhaps hurricanes making landfall in the United States is a part of fulfilling those prophecies. If you view what is happening within our political system as a great shaking, as I do, then the unease of North Korea's actions that is shaking its neighbors, world unrest focused on the Middle East, earthquakes, fires, hurricanes, and other natural disasters are all signs of the fulfilling of prophecy. And I do not have a sense that these prophecies have been completely fulfilled yet.

When prayers lifted to God include "whatever it takes," we can be sure that all-knowing God already knows what it is going to take. He is not guessing about what might work; rather, He knows what will work, and He is working His plan.

Lord God Almighty, help us as a nation, culture, and people to quickly recognize that you not only want our attention, but you also want our lives given to you. May we quickly see that You alone are our only hope and salvation. May we turn to You as our Lord and Savior. You, O God, know what it will take for America to do so, and we place our trust and faith in You. Lord God, in Your boundless mercy, protect those who are in harm's way, in Jesus's name.

September 16

Our Groaning Earth

Romans 8:18–25

Harvey and Irma are quite a pair. Harvey contained millions of acre feet of water, while Irma contained winds approaching 200 miles per hour. Both proved to be very destructive to nature and man-made objects. I sense that in nature itself, the earth is groaning, as God's creation races toward the end of the age.

Let me say it like this: our hope is not in this world or the things created. Our hope is in the Creator, the Triune God, Father, Son, and Holy Spirit. He alone is my refuge, my place of safety, my shelter, my comfort, my joy, and my peace. John ends the book of Revelation with these words: "Even so come Lord Jesus." Our hope lies not in a world and nature that corrects itself. Our hope is in the soon return of Jesus Christ. Even so, come Lord Jesus.

September 17

Watching the Weather

Luke 21:25

Some nine million people have been impacted by Hurricane Harvey, and now some eighteen million have been impacted by Hurricane Irma. In a two-week period, over 8 percent of the US population has had some impact from hurricane damage. I am not predicting this, but could the next impactful event occur the weekend of September 23 as another major hurricane is predicted to hit the Southeast of the United States, and perhaps involve over thirty-six million people? Nine—eighteen—thirty-six? I think we must be cognizant of these far-reaching and economic impact points. Estimates are that property damage and economic losses will amount to close to $75 billion, just from Harvey alone, and perhaps double that for Irma. I do not write this as a worry factor but to simply say that it will be important to be watchful as our world races toward the appointed time of Jesus Christ's return.

I believe that God's Word plainly points out that we, as Christians, are to *watch* as we are waiting. Watching does not ignore what is happening in disasters or other catastrophic events; rather, watching puts us in a place of expectancy to prepare for coming days. I'm waiting for the trumpet of God to sound at any moment. While I am waiting, I am keeping a watchful eye on what our world is facing, and again I say, "Even so, come Lord Jesus."

September 18

Regretting My Actions

Luke 22:54–62

All four of the Gospel writers of the New Testament capture the scene and story of Peter's denying that he even knew Jesus, three times in a short time in the early morning of Jesus's crucifixion. The man who was willing to fight with a sword just a short time earlier was now cold, confused, and confounded. The one whom Peter had watched perform countless miracles was allowing Himself to be beaten and face certain death. In this confused state, Peter denied Jesus three times, and then a rooster crowed for the second time, and Peter suddenly remembered that what Jesus had told him earlier that evening had just come to pass.

God's Word records that Peter wept bitterly. This was not just a portrayal of sorrow or grief. This was inconsolable weeping of remorse, regret, and torment of what Peter had done. I have observed that those who come to an altar of salvation sometimes will weep in a similar manner as Jesus washes away the sin in their lives. Peter would soon repent of this and receive Jesus's forgiveness. He would go on to be the first to boldly proclaim the Gospel on the day of Pentecost.

Jesus can take you from the worst of situations and bring you to complete victory in the briefest of time. Jesus desires to do that for you today. Just let Him as you weep in His presence.

God Wants All of You

2 Corinthians 6:4

God makes it abundantly clear in His Word that He wants our all—all our lives, including the mess we have made of it; all our souls; all our hearts; all our beings. God wants all of it—not just a portion but all of it.

When it comes to each one of us and God wanting our all, God describes Himself as a jealous God. The thought here is that God does not want to share us with anyone else. That may be hard to understand from a human viewpoint. but it might be understood best by looking at the biblical perspective of marriage—one man to only one wife in a pure relationship.

When I knew that LaDonna was my one and only, I had jealous thoughts toward any other guy who I thought was looking at my future wife with intent to lure her away. She was mine, and I didn't want anyone else trying to take her. I wanted her all, and God blessed me with exactly that.

We can't just give God a portion of ourselves and call it good. No, God wants it all. I am not a good sharer regarding dessert. Sometimes LaDonna will ask me if I just want to share a dessert after a meal out, and sometimes I reluctantly agree. But most of the time, I want all of it. The whole thing, and not just part. I want the whole piece of apple pie with two large scoops of ice cream. I want it all for myself.

God is that way with us. He wants all and does not like to share. Give God your all. Let a jealous God gather you in His arms and love you today.

Deception—A Treacherous Path

1 Timothy 4:1–5

My Bible reading this morning led me to some intriguing insight into my personal life. I have never been one to be picky about what I eat. I was raised on a farm, and we ate fresh produce from our garden. We ate beef, chicken, and pork that was raised on our farm, some of which we butchered ourselves. We raised wheat, but flour was so cheap in the store that we did not grind our own. My grandparents milked enough cows to be able to sell milk and cream to the creamery in town. We raised enough chickens to sell their eggs as well.

Our world culture has advanced from well over 50 percent of the US population involved in production agriculture, to today, with less than 2 percent of the population producing enough food and fiber to feed us, as well as to contribute significantly to a hungry world; great change has taken place.

With today's safety standards in place, the foods that we consume are delicious, free of parasites, safe, and nutritious. The use of technology has allowed less than 2 percent of our national population to be prolific in what they do. Unfortunately, there is an effort, perhaps even a cult, in our world that preaches that everything that isn't organic, or non-GMO, is harmful and will kill us.

I am going to be bold and will undoubtedly step on some toes, but I share by the authority of God's Word that says,

> Now the Holy Spirit tells us clearly that in the last times some will turn away from the true faith; they will follow deceptive spirits and teachings that come from demons. These people are hypocrites and liars, and their consciences are dead. They will say it is wrong to be married and wrong to eat certain

> foods. But God created those foods to be eaten with thanks by faithful people who know the truth. Since everything God created is good, we should not reject any of it but receive it with thanks. For we know it is made acceptable by the word of God and prayer. (1 Timothy 4:1–5 NLT)

With thanksgiving, I will enjoy my sweet corn that has been engineered to protect against ear worm. I will eat pork that, with the use of modern science, is free from parasites. I will utilize crops that are designed to be safe on the environment, to feed livestock that will produce the very nice ribeye steaks that I enjoy; livestock that will also produce the delicious, nutritious milk for large dairies, where I am able to buy it at a reasonable price—milk that is used to make the wonderful ice cream that I enjoy.

If you desire to eat differently than I do, that is fine, but if you are in the group that says that my choice of food is wrong, then you are with the wrong crowd. Don't be misled by deceptive spirits and teachings. That, my friends, is God's Word.

September 21

A Devouring Enemy

1 Peter 5:8

While you were sleeping, God was not. We have a human understanding that God is present everywhere, all the time, and that is true.

God's Word also tells us that the same is not true about the enemy of our souls, Satan. The Bible says that he goes to and fro on this earth, and as I see the end of this age quickly unfolding, I believe that Satan is in a frenzy in his efforts.

Don't be caught up in Satan's frenzy. Recognize that God is present with you today as you walk life's path.

God walking with you. *Wow!*

September 22

No Sun Needed

Revelation 21:22-27

Fall starts today. The sun rose and will set smack-dab in the middle of any true east/west road or street, making it difficult to see as the sun shines in your face. The Bible shares with us that in heaven, there will be no need of the sun because the light proceeding from God's throne will be more than adequate—brilliance beyond description. That's what awaits us in heaven. It's an unimaginable life for all who go there. I want to be sure to be there. The requirement is that Jesus has forgiven me of my sins, washed them all away, and He lives in my heart and life. Make sure that is true in your life, today and every day.

September 23

Victory Is Mine

1 Corinthians 15:57

God's plan includes me, and it includes you as well. God's Word confirms that His plan for our lives is for good and not evil. Then why does evil infringe on our lives—lives that are planned by God? Perhaps it's because God wants us to know His power and the victory over evil that He brings.

God has influences over our entire beings, and that influence can lead us to victory over any evil that comes our way.

Are you battling some evil? God has a victory in store for you, a victory over that evil. God has never lost a battle, and He is not about to start with a little problem like mine or yours.

Victory is ours today, in the name of Jesus.

September 24

Hot Out of the Oven

Isaiah 28:10

For me, a great meal must be accompanied by a soft, plump, hot-from-the-oven, freshly baked yeast roll, held and eaten with my left hand while wielding a dinner fork in my right. But a roll doesn't just appear out of nowhere.

I have watched as my wife, LaDonna, and her staff create these wonderful, delectable dinner rolls. It's amazing the results they get from just a few simple ingredients. But they must follow a recipe to achieve these wonderful delights.

The ingredients are simple: flour, salt, yeast, and warm water—and a hot oven. These ingredients, used in the right combination, in the right sequence, and prepared properly, yield a wonderful-tasting roll. If you bake the flour without mixing all the other ingredients together, you have great failure. If you use cold water to dissolve the yeast, you have failure. If you just plop the dough in one great big pile and throw it in the oven, you have failure. Success only occurs when you place all the ingredients together, in sequence and in the right proportions; form the right-sized portions by hand; place them into a hot oven; and take them out at the proper time.

I have found that I sometimes want to get things done without going through the proper sequence. I want to get out of the heat before I am completely done. I don't like the warm water; I either want cold or hot. I want to throw part of my life in the oven without adding the other ingredients that God desires to place in my life.

God is creating a unique end-product with ingredients that He is mixing into our lives. He is a master chef when it comes to preparing individuals for the work He wants us to do in His kingdom.

God, continue to do your work in my life. I want to be like a piece of wonderful, delightful bread in the lives of others today.

September 25

Positive Words

James 3:10

In this negative world we live in, I choose to speak blessing into the lives of others. No one is perfect, and we can easily find fault and pick people apart like vultures, but I choose instead to speak blessing.

We talk so much about the negative things shared as news by the media. Consider that the people giving the news were raised in a negative environment. Consider that they were brought up without any positive influence in their lives, and now we listen, as they spew the vomit of negativism.

Friends, it's our delight to find the good in others. Speak good and goodness into their lives. Build them up with encouragement and support for the good in their lives. Speaking good into the lives of others brings about positive change, especially in the one speaking the positive words.

Want to make a change for the better? That is as easy as speaking positive words to someone who needs to hear them.

Low-Hanging Fruit

Psalm 21:8–13

Sin and evil often hide themselves by looking good.

A few years ago, while driving on a quiet street in a suburb of Phoenix, Arizona, we passed under some orange trees whose fruit was hanging low enough to just reach out the window of the vehicle and pick it. In fact, the street was completely lined with these trees, loaded with wonderful, lush, ripe oranges, just right for picking. I stopped the vehicle, reached out, and plucked one of those wonderful fruits right off the tree. As I brought the fruit inside the van and rolled up the window, the fragrance of citrus orange filled the vehicle with a wonderful perfume, and when I started to peel the fruit, the fragrance exploded into the vehicle. I couldn't wait to place some of that wonderful fruit into my mouth, finally satisfying my desire to taste the fruit that was giving off such a wonderful fragrance.

I opened the orange, peeled off a slice, and popped it into my mouth. The juice immediately gushed forth and filled my mouth—with the most bitter-tasting citric acid I have ever encountered. It made my mouth pucker, and I quickly rolled down the window and spit out what I could. That was my first experience with an ornamental orange—and my last.

Sin and evil often take on similar characteristics. Looks good, feels good, even smells good, but once you get a taste, you recognize it for what it is. By faith, I can expect God to keep me from evil and sin because He leads me in paths of righteousness.

The fruit of evil may hang over my head and be appealing, but I can choose to drive right on by. I no longer pick oranges from low-hanging branches. I have learned my lesson.

September 27

A Whole Lot of Shaking

Hebrews 12:27–29

If you have listened to Christian news, preaching, or interaction in the past few months, you might have noticed a lot of emphasis on a worldwide "shaking" that is soon to happen. My Bible reading this morning reinforces those prophecies and words of knowledge.

"When God spoke from Mount Sinai his voice shook the earth, but now he makes another promise: 'Once again I will shake not only the earth but the heavens also." Hebrews 12:26 New Living Translation) This means that all of creation will be shaken and removed, so that only unshakable things will remain. Since we are receiving a kingdom that is unshakable, let us be thankful and please God by worshiping him with holy fear and awe. "For our God is a devouring fire". (Hebrews 12: 29 New Living Translation)

I desire to know that my faith is unshakable. How do I get to that place? By consuming God's Word, being thankful, and pleasing God by worshiping Him with holy fear and awe.

I do not know what this shaking will be like. I only know that God's Word is pure truth, and God gives warning of what He is preparing to do. A shaking is coming that the world and the heavens have never experienced. And my faith must be unshakable.

September 28

Simply Amazing

1 Corinthians 15:10

To say that I am amazed by God is an understatement. I have experienced jaw-dropping, mind-whirling, life-changing, and clearly miraculous acts of God in my life. First and foremost is my personal salvation. That God, as a man, would die on a cross, giving up His blood and life to atone for my sin, is amazing. His sacrifice was applied to my life years ago and is still present in my life today. That is amazing.

That God would protect me from harm when it came my way amazes me. That God, the Creator of all that is known and all that is unknown to man, would desire to talk to me personally and individually absolutely amazes me. That over forty-eight years ago God gave me a godly woman to be my wife and companion, who gave us children and grandchildren, is truly amazing. That God would lead me to participate in missions trips these last ten years is totally amazing.

Amazing God, you're still amazing me today, and I find that *amazing*!

September 29

A Godly Life
2 Peter 1:3

Living a godly life is a commitment. Second Peter 1:3 says,

> By his divine power, God has given us everything we need for living a godly life. We have received all of this by coming to know him, the one who called us to himself by means of his marvelous glory and excellence. (NLT)

A key phrase in this scripture is "everything we need." I often tackle home plumbing projects. As I start working, I usually discover that I don't have a needed part or component, which requires me to make a trip to the hardware store. After two or three more trips to get everything I need, I finish the project. How much easier it would have been if I had had everything I needed when I started.

No matter where you are in your Christian walk, God has already provided everything you need to live a godly life. I believe that God desires that we take full advantage of that supply.

The old chorus says, "He's all I need; He's all I need; Jesus is all I need."

That, my friend, is truth.

September 30

Authority

Matthew 17:20

Authority is a powerful tool and weapon. When God created Adam and Eve, he gave them dominion, or authority, over all the creation that He had created in the six days previous. That authority included the plants and animals and the fish of the sea.

As the culture of humankind advanced, God gave authority to rulers and governments. When God the Son, Jesus Christ, became man in the flesh, He was given all authority from the Father, God. During the recorded events of Jesus's ministry, we find that he exercised this authority many, many times.

Just before Jesus ascended into heaven to sit at the right hand of the Father, He told the disciples that He was giving them all the authority that they had seen in Him and even more. That authority was described in God's Word in this way: "If you have faith as small as a mustard seed you can say to this mountain, 'be moved from here to there' and it will move" (Mathew 17: 20 New International Version)

Too often in our Christian culture, we are waiting for God to do something "big" for us, when, in fact, He has already given us authority that goes beyond what we saw exercised while Jesus was living here on this earth. It's just a matter of the size of our faith.

Our faith does not have to be as large as the mountain. A mustard seed is approximately 0.05 inches in diameter. In other words, you could line up twenty mustard seeds in a one-inch length of space.

I live on the Plains of the United States. The nearest tall mountain is about three hundred miles away. It's called Pike's Peak. This mountain contains dozens of square miles of rock and dirt. How much faith does it take to move a literal mountain? That little mustard seed dropped from a plane onto Pike's Peak would never be found, but faith in that volume can move mountains.

I think God tires of our constantly coming to Him with our problems and mountains when He has given us authority over those things. My faith is built up and increased by reading and hearing God's Word. I want my faith to be at least as large as a mustard seed.

What would happen if you had mustard-seed faith in your life? Jesus said you could.

October 1

Pastors—God's Gift to the Church

Ephesians 4:11-13

October is designated as Pastor or Clergy Appreciation month. The apostle Paul shares the following:

> Now these are the gifts Christ gave to the church: the apostles, the prophets, the evangelists, and the pastors and teachers. Their responsibility is to equip God's people to do his work and build up the church, the body of Christ. This will continue

> until we all come to such unity in our faith and knowledge of God's Son that we will be mature in the Lord, measuring up to the full and complete standard of Christ. (Ephesians 4:11–13)

Within my church and yours as well reside gifts of God in the manner described above. These are an incredible gifts to the church, and I have the privilege of knowing individuals who are truly those who are described in all five of these gifts. Appreciation can be shown in many ways. It's always easy to allow your church to do something that represents the congregation, but I am challenged in my life to do something in appreciation for those I know are mentioned above. Something done personally and in an appropriate manner is always in good taste. Let's all do the things that we can to show appreciation in October to those who help build the kingdom of God. Make sure your congregation shows their appreciation, but also make sure your personal appreciation is shown too.

October 2

Really Big God

Revelation 5:11–14; 21:15–21

My Bible reading for the next few days will take me into the book of Revelation. John, the writer of Revelation, describes some very large things and numbers that he was shown as he was taken on a tour of God's throne room. He was also shown many things that were to come. One of the things he saw was a large group of angels whose voices, in "mighty chorus," were singing, "Worthy is the Lamb who was slaughtered to receive power and riches and wisdom and strength and honor and glory and blessing." The number of these angels is given as "thousands and millions."

I know that God cares very much for the little things in our lives, and He is moved by the things that we experience. He cares deeply for us as we deal with these small things. But John gives us a description of a God who enjoys "big stuff." Huge crowds of angels and people, a huge book that contains the name of every person who has given his or her heart to God, and a huge heaven, some fourteen hundred miles square and deep, are just a few of the big things John saw.

I know that I'll need to adjust a little to live in a huge place like heaven. Currently, I think a city spread over a ten-square-mile area is too large for me to adjust. Heaven is big. God is even bigger. If God did all that John saw, then I must know that He can do *mighty things* in my life.

I think God loves to do things in a big way. I can't let the little things discourage me as I share them with a holy God. My God can crush the little things to powder and show me great and mighty things, too wonderful to describe. I am overwhelmed because He desires to do that for little ol' me. And I know that He desires to do that for you as well.

Lord God Almighty, we desire to see the bigness of Your power and might as You live through us.

October 3

Different Is Good—Servanthood

Mark 10:42–45

As Christians who know that we should be doing something for the Lord, I think we often struggle with what that *something* should be. We struggle with a mind-set that is persuaded that we can never be a Billy Graham, a well-known missionary, a successful pastor of a church you know, or even a Sunday school teacher you admire. This I have discovered as I have served God: He made me to be different than any other individual serving God. The uniqueness that God gave each of us was intended to be used in uniqueness in the kingdom of God. I know many pastors, and not one of them has a ministry that is exactly like another's. I have met many Sunday school teachers, and not one of them has an identical teaching skill as another.

We are unique, and God created us that way. You may say, "I know that I am not called to be a missionary, pastor, or teacher," and I believe you, as God does not call everyone to be a missionary, pastor, or teacher. But this I believe: when Jesus gave me His salvation, and I accepted Jesus into my heart, He placed a calling to serve in my life.

Some of us will preach and teach, but most will not be on the platform or at the teacher's podium. What should your role be? To be like Jesus. Jesus said of Himself, *I didn't come to be served. Rather, I came to serve.* That is a great place to start—serve. Where can you start? Maybe you can take a class of wiggly, bouncy juniors out for ice cream with their teachers. Maybe you can bring some snacks to the youth services for them to enjoy while they have service. Maybe you can take a sack of groceries to a single mom with kids who is struggling to make ends meet. I could list hundreds of things where you could serve and never exhaust the needs.

If you know in your heart that you are not doing as much as you think God would have you do, start by simply asking God, "What do you want me to do today to serve others?" I have found that when I ask God that question, He opens doors and windows of opportunity, and it's up to me to take those opportunities and serve. When I serve others, I am patterning my life after Jesus. Serving is a God calling with which every one of us can be involved. And who knows? God may expand your calling into areas you never dreamed of. It doesn't get any more exciting than that, friends. Serve!

October 4

A Directed Path for a Sunday

Proverbs 3:1–6

It is not coincidence that God has brought all of us to this point and has placed us where we are. Whether blessed or in need, God has directed our paths. You are not reading these words by mere chance or coincidence; rather, I believe that God has divinely appointed your steps to include this reading. It is easy to look back and see what was or even what could have been. But it is also easy to look forward, looking beyond our current circumstances and simply trust God.

Your response may be, "But I don't know what God would have me do." I have found that I can trust God with today and all my tomorrows. Will God stretch me? It's likely. If you are like me, your physical body needs to stretch from time to time. Our spiritual lives likely are similar. But I can trust God, the master sports trainer, to stretch me without injury. Today, perhaps the stretching that God wants for you is to attend church. Do it. If the doors fall off the church when you enter, they can be repaired, and what a story you will have to share with friends and family.

But seriously, God is saying to us, get up, get ready, and go to My house. He will meet us there and minister to our lives things which we cannot fully understand or explain. The Lord God of heaven and earth, desires to meet with His people, pour out His Spirit upon us, and satisfy the desire and hunger of our souls.

I'm headed to church in a few minutes. See you there, but most importantly, God will meet us there.

Two Equals One
Genesis 2:24

God makes an intriguing statement in Genesis 2:24—"Therefore shall a man leave his father and mother and cleave unto his wife: and they shall be one flesh" (KJV). *One flesh* has long captivated my attention. Certainly, the reference is speaking of marriage between a man and a woman and the sexual union and relationship that occurs within that marriage. I love that as we gain scientific knowledge in our modern world, it continues to prove and provide insight into what God spoke thousands of years ago.

Scientists have recently found that many female brains contain nonrelated male DNA, and in many cases, several different nonrelated male DNA. While still being researched, it appears that the transfer of male sperm and seminal fluid to any part of the female body that can absorb allows DNA to be transferred into the female body, and it accumulates in the brain. If there are multiple partners, there is found to be multiple DNA.

For my entire life, I have felt and firmly believed, based on biblical principles, that sex is a lifetime commitment between just one man and one woman in a marriage relationship. Science is helping to prove God's Word to be truthful and infallible. God's way—proving once again to be best.

October 6

A Wrestling Match

Ephesians 6:10–18

What makes something a really big deal? Sometimes, it's something extremely small, like a pin prick in a balloon or one extra digit in a phone number. The enemy of our souls loves to start his charades in almost-unnoticed small things. As Christians, we must always have a clear understanding that Satan's entire purpose is to hurt, kill, and destroy. Just as a balloon filled with helium is destroyed by one very small pin prick, so our lives can be destroyed by Satan's evil plans.

God's desire is to walk beside each of us, even carrying us, if needed, and blessing our lives with His presence. Satan's plan is to burst that bubble and then try to make you think it is God's fault. Friends, that's a big deal in my estimation. We must recognize that we wrestle not against flesh and blood but against principalities (of which we know little) and rulers of darkness, against which in our human selves have no power.

We must have the power of almighty God, living in and through us in Jesus Christ, to recognize the work of Satan. He is an expert at making destruction, spiritual death, and all sin look enticing. As Christians, we must use God's Spirit to discern the evil disguised as something good that lurks around us. Evil is just a sharp pin ready to burst your balloon.

Which Path?

Matthew 7:13–14

Two paths to choose: one you win; one you lose. Your choice makes a difference. God's desire for you is not to lose.

Life is often referred to as a path. There are two paths described in God's Word: one leads to eternal life in God's heaven, and one leads to eternal damnation in hell. On God's path, you win; on the other path, you lose. God grants us the ability to decide which path we follow. If you are unsure of which path you're on, or if you know that you're on the path to destruction, you can choose to be certain that you are on the path to eternal life in God's heaven.

I cannot make the decision for you, but I can encourage you to make your own decision to follow Jesus. Our Savior makes it very simple. Acknowledge that you are not sure of the path you're on, or you know for certain that you are not on the right path. Ask Jesus to forgive you of all the sin in your life, and with God's help, repent and turn away from that sin.

God's Word says, "Believe on the Lord Jesus Christ and thou shalt be saved, and thy house." (Acts 16:31 AKJV) It's that simple. Do it now and know you are on the path to eternal life with Jesus.

Two paths to walk: one you win; one you lose. God's Word says, "and thine ears shall hear a word behind thee, saying, This is the way, walk ye in it, when ye turn to the right hand and when ye turn to the left" (Isaiah 30:21 AKJV)

Your choice to walk His way makes all the difference. God desires for you to be sure and to win.

The Wind of the Holy Spirit

John 3:8

Our driving yesterday took us alongside some wind turbine farms, spinning in a gentle Kansas wind (less than twenty-five miles per hour). While driving, I was thinking about what God is planning for the center of this great nation. I believe that God has a great outpouring that is going to occur and I was contemplating the role I and others would play in seeing this come to pass and the importance that where I live is going to have involving a great outpouring of God's Holy Spirit. I was reminded of the wind of the Holy Spirit. The area in which we live, the High Plains of America, has perfect conditions for wind turbines, as the wind blows a large percent of the time. The difference between here and other places in the world that have wind is that the wind in the Plains blows from the north, south, east, and west. I have, on occasion, observed the wind changing directions throughout the course of the day and blowing from a full 360 degrees during a twenty-four-hour period.

God's Holy Spirit nudged me and spoke this into my heart and soul: *"I am about to allow my Spirit to blow like the wind from every direction and cover your land with my presence."* Just looking out the windshield, I could not see the wind or even feel it, but I could certainly see the evidence as the turbines turned in the wind. Those turbines are made to turn a full 360 degrees and catch the wind from any direction.

Almighty God, allow me to be like those turbines and catch the wind of Your Holy Spirit. Allow me to generate Your presence wherever I go. Holy Spirit Outpouring. God, your will is all I long for.

Am I a Faith Hero

Hebrews 11:1–40

Faith itself and acts of faith are limitless. God's Word is full of life stories of men and women of faith and acts of faith that are evidence of the power of God working in miraculous ways. When asked what faith is, we are quick to point out the biblical definition and key in on specific scripture. We have the pat answer, but do we possess the real thing in our everyday lives? In some instances, yes, but in many cases, no. Why did those who were listed in the "Hall of Faith" chapter in Hebrews 11 get that notoriety? It was because they lived their lives completely in faith and not just partially. In many cases, the promises that God gave to these individuals was not fully realized in their lifetimes, and in some cases, God's promise is still unfolding.

Faith is recognizing that God speaks truth, and when He speaks to you and me directly, we can believe it, count on it, accept it, trust in it, and watch God unfold it in our lives. Perhaps it will not get completely unfolded in our lifetimes, but by faith, our descendants will see the fulfillment of God's promises to us. Faith is never giving up hope, watching diligently for the pieces to come together, and waiting expectantly, though sometimes impatiently, for God to do His part.

Our part in the meantime? Believe, without doubt, God's Word, God's promises, God's limitless ability, and God's power. Through Him, all things are possible. Let your faith increase by reading and letting God's Word build your faith.

I read Jesus's words just before He went to heaven to sit at the right hand of the Father. He promised that all the things His disciples had seen Him do, they would do and even more. By faith, I am going to see that happen in my life and the lives of other disciples. By faith, I receive Jesus's promise for my life.

Ready or Not, Here I Come

1 Thessalonians 4:16–18

I believe that we should live our lives with an understanding that Jesus could take His church out of this world at any time or that our lives here on earth could end at any moment. The only thing keeping Jesus from taking His people home is that God has not yet given the command. All signs point to that command being given at any time, and I, for one, want to be ready. How do I know that I am ready for the trumpet of God to sound? By knowing with assurance that my name is written in the Lamb's book of life. I have asked Jesus to come into my heart, cleanse me from sin, and make me a new person. That was not just a one-time deal and then I went on with a sinful life. Paul the apostle says in essence: I die daily to the sins of this world. In other words, I renew my commitment to God each day—sometimes several times a day—asking for and accepting His grace and forgiveness for any sin that has entered my life and choosing to flee from that sin.

One of these days—and I believe it will be soon—that trumpet will sound. I want to know that I am ready to go. Of all the trips and travel that I have been blessed to experience, that's the ultimate trip I am waiting for. Jesus is telling us, *"Ready or not, here I come."* Let's be ready!

October 11

Condemnation—A Tool of the Devil

John 3:14–21

Condemnation on this side of eternity is a ploy of the devil. His motive is to place you under condemnation while you are living here on earth so that there will be condemnation for an eternal reward. Jesus Christ offers hope, restoration, peace, and joy, and instead of condemnation, Jesus offers forgiveness. Condemnation or forgiveness? It's your choice.

Mistakes and sin enter our lives even as Christians. Yes, but forgiveness is offered without regard. Cast all your cares and your sin at Jesus's feet and confess your sin. Jesus is faithful and just and will forgive you of your sin. All the enemy of your soul can offer is condemnation. Forgiveness is a free gift from God.

Let Jesus break the chains of condemnation right now—today. You have been bound long enough. Let Jesus's forgiveness set you free; it's simple. Tell Jesus you are tired of condemnation and you want to be set free. Confess your sins, and ask Jesus to forgive you. As you do that, you will feel the presence of a holy God forgiving you and setting you free. Do it today. You have experienced enough condemnation. Jesus Christ, the Son of God, offers forgiveness.

October 12

God's Word—Infallible

2 Timothy 3:14–17

I believe that God's Word, the Holy Bible, is the infallible (dependable, unfailing, reliable, fail-safe, trustworthy, certain, flawless, and foolproof) and inerrant (containing no errors, incapable of being in error) message that God wanted communicated with all of humankind. Many translations that have been released since Moses wrote the first five books of the Old Testament have tried to capture the full meaning of the original writing, and sometimes th original meaning is changed or lost. Though that may be the case, I have a deep assurance that, as time has moved forward, the full intent and impact of God's Word has been maintained in integrity and meaning. The underlying theme of the Holy Bible, God's Word, is God's plan of redemption and salvation. At the end of this physical life on earth, each of us will enter eternal destiny.

God's Word declares with authority that only those whose names are found in the Lamb's book of life—the book that is in God's hands, with entries made only by the three-person Godhead—will experience eternal life in heaven. That's God's Word—infallible and inerrant. I don't decide that for anyone else but me, and you can't decide for anyone else but you. My name is there. Is yours?

October 13

Fake News—Vomit on Display

Proverbs 26:11–12

I have a great dislike for those who spew only bad news and fake news. Our world media today, in my opinion, needs their mouths washed out with lye soap, their pants dropped, and their backsides beaten with a strong willow switch. This activity is a plague that is worse than any virus or disease that has claimed the lives of thousands or even millions in recent decades. The sad part is that we know it is happening, and we do nothing about it.

Modern technology allows us to generate a five- to seven-second sound bite, most often taken completely out of context, and repeated until we are brainwashed. I don't watch national news because I get riled at the lies and half-truths spewed as vomit across our world, and there is nothing that turns my stomach worse than vomit, media or otherwise. And yet as a nation, we fill our lives with the hatred and vomit every time we turn on our news.

God's Word speaks very clearly regarding what we allow to be broadcast as news—"like a dog returneth to his vomit." (Proverbs 26:11 AKJV)

I can pray that things get better, but I need to lift my voice along with others to demand integrity in media news. I probably am in the minority, but look at what other insignificant minority groups have done in recent years. I'm headed out to buy some lye soap and cut a willow switch or two. I think both will be useful.

October 14

Scars—Signs of the Past

Isaiah 53:1–12

Today, our painting crew, led by Cynthia K. will complete the interior painting of our church parsonage. We are thankful to all the volunteers who made this happen. The interior walls have housed people for well over fifty years, and as with any house that is lived in, the walls get scuffed and marred. That's a normal thing as life occurs within the walls of any home. If only those walls could talk! What a history they could provide.

As we painted, we filled nail holes and covered over some marred areas, making them look new again. The scars are still on the wall but hidden from view with a new coat of paint. When Jesus comes into a life, it is like a coat of paint. The scars of life are there, but Jesus comes into our lives and covers us (paints) with His blood, and we are fresh and new once again. The blemishes are covered over, and we can begin anew.

The walls of our lives will most likely get scuffed and marred again, but Jesus's blood never runs out, for there is a vast supply. Let

Jesus's blood cover your life and past. Old things are passed away; behold, all things are new. That's God's Word—the Master Painter.

We are excited to have life once again within the walls of our parsonage, waiting for all the activity that will take place there.

October 15

World Volatility

John 16:29–33

It is obvious that the world can revolve from a day of some stability to a day of instability. The 2016 voting in Europe has once again shown the volatility with which our world lives. I do not pretend to know exactly what the future holds, but I believe that world volatility will escalate in these last days before the church of Jesus Christ is taken away. At least one thing will help us stand in stability during these days of instability. That one thing is the calm assurance that Jesus Christ is living in and through our lives and that the Word of God is a solid foundation.

Worry and despair will control many and will cause unstableness. Godly men and women living in the stability of Jesus Christ must be an anchor for others to hold.

Lord God Almighty, You are my anchor. May the world around me see stability as I trust in You alone.

Sin Is Attractive but Deadly

Proverbs 19:12; 20:1

Why does God list as sin, which separates us from God, those things that are attractive to us, are enticing, and are downright enjoyable? It is because of the unseen and unknown impact and results. Why does an adult keep a toddler from touching that bright pot on a hot stove? It's because the adult knows what will happen if the toddler touches the hot pot.

I have a cousin who spilled hot liquid from a pot on the stove onto himself when he was very young, giving him severe burns. I'm sure the shiny pot on the stove looked attractive to him at the time but resulted in unwanted pain and suffering. Why does God's Word speak out plainly about the use of alcohol? Because of the unknown impact. How many people are killed in highway accidents, how many homes are broken, and how much physical abuse occurs because of alcohol? Far too many—and even one is too many. You might say that you can control yourself and your alcohol consumption. God's Word says that alcohol and strong drink is a mocker and a mockery to God. Consuming alcohol is simply trying to tell God, with complete failure, that you know better than He does. There is far too much unknown that is a result of alcohol consumption. It's perhaps attractive from a peer-pressure standpoint, but you cannot know the fullness of the result of allowing alcohol into your life.

God's Word is clearly incapable of error. I trust what God says. You can make excuse, but I am concerned what will your answer be when you stand before God Almighty and give an account.

October 17

A Good Diet

John 6:47–51

I love to eat, and my body shows it, as I'm a little overweight. Our bodies signal the need to eat with hunger pangs. Most of us have experienced a busy day, when we have delayed eating, and suddenly, the hunger pangs say that we must do something. And what do we do? Get something to eat, of course.

Our spiritual bodies are made in a similar fashion. There is a place within our beings that only God can fill. The enemy of our souls will try to convince us that this place can be filled with the things of this world, but those things will never, ever satisfy the "hunger" that God creates for this, His place. How, then, do I satisfy this hunger? I'm glad you asked.

The things of this world can be pictured as water running through a sieve. The sieve gets wet, but nothing sticks. But then we allow God to fill that place reserved for Him, and the "substance" of God stays in place and satisfies the hunger. With human food, many things are made with a recipe, and when followed, we have a great food item that is wonderful and very tasty. While there is no recipe for filling the God place within our lives, there are things that contribute to allowing God to do so.

First, as God speaks to us, we must recognize that, in fact, God is speaking, and He is speaking directly to us. We may need to push some things out of our lives to make room for God. I willingly do so because I have found the benefit of having God fill His place in my life. We can allow God to fill this, His rightful place, by reading the Holy Bible and meditating upon what is said in His Word. We can pray with words that come from the heart. God is a communicator. Not only does He hear us when we pray, but He is willing to carry on a conversation with each one of us—and when He speaks, He speaks truth.

Give God the opportunity to speak directly to you. As you allow God to take His rightful place in your life, you will discover that you will willingly enlarge the place that is His. For me, I enjoy His companionship and presence. I desire to make for Him a dwelling place within my life and to allow God to fill that place that only He can fill.

October 18

Passiveness or Compassion

Matthew 9:35–38

Passiveness is an easy road when it's someone else's problem, sickness, pain, or suffering. Other than Jesus's cruel crucifixion and death, God's Word does not indicate that Jesus suffered any illness or injury. His human nature could have easily been passive as He encountered people—many, many people who had needs. Here is the difference in Jesus—He had compassion for them. Jesus set passiveness aside and let compassion become the driving force in His life.

Many people encounter a tough life through no fault of their own. When Jesus encountered these folks, He was moved with compassion. My compassion level is not at the level of Jesus's. Lord, let my compassion be like Jesus's, that I will minister to those in need in the same way Jesus would minister. Let me see humanity as You see us, with all our sickness, disease, problems, and life's burdens. And then let me be moved with compassion in a similar manner in which You were moved. Amen.

October 19

Intuitive Help

Romans 8:26–28

Modern electronics help to make life easier. A message comes on in my truck to check the brake control system, and sure enough, I have no brakes to the trailer. Fortunately, it was just that a relay had tripped and needed to be reset. And that was easy; just turn the truck off for a few seconds, and it automatically reset. God often sends us messages through His Word, His anointed messenger, or His Holy Spirit. The best thing to do is check to see if the message is accurate, and then take the necessary actions to correct what is wrong.

God has a perfect record of being right. I'm glad that the fix my truck needed was simple, but even if it wasn't, I'm thankful for the warning. I'm thankful that God cares enough about me and you that He gives us warning. Don't ignore His warnings—they are true and accurate. Do what is necessary to correct what is wrong. God, the Master Mechanic, is waiting to help you.

October 20

Life Is Short

James 4:13–17

Our community has been reminded again of the brevity of life on this earth. In human estimation, it was a life that was snuffed out much too young, a life that was contributing to family, society, community, and much more. The possibilities that were the future are now altered and have become what could have been. We all have a past; some of that past is really good, and some of it is not so good or perhaps even dark.

We now live in the present, and all of us have plans for tomorrow, next week, next month, next year, and well into the future. I'm well into my sixties, and it would be easy for me to develop a forty-year plan. But my next breath is not guaranteed. I'm promised only this breath, and so what I do with this breath, this moment, this instant in life, must count for eternity. God's Word tells us that each of us has an appointed time to experience earthly death, and then we will be judged for our works. Standing before a judge—any judge—is not appealing to me, but by the laws of this land, when I am called into a court of law, I must show up and answer the questions that are submitted to me.

God's Word says that everyone, will stand before God Almighty and give an account for our lives here on earth. It will be a factual account, with no twists or half-truths. With this breath, this moment, I have an opportunity to do something that will be judged for eternity.

Lord God Almighty, help me live a live that is pleasing to You—this moment, with this breath.

October 21

Depraved and Reprobate Mind

2 Timothy 3:1–9

Deprave, depraved, and depravity are words that are not commonly used in our conversations, and you don't hear them spoken by mainstream media. Deprave means corrupt, debauch, degrade, defile or pollute. Depravity means corruption, degradation, vice, or perversion. No wonder we don't use these words because we are all good people, without sin (or very little sin). We have our own righteousness and are proud to stand up and affirm our own righteousness, pointing at someone else and accusing them of being less righteous than we are.

The apostle Paul, in his second letter to Timothy, referred to some of the teachers and leaders of that day as having depraved minds and a counterfeit faith. Let me speak plainly: our world—whether society, government, world and national leaders, and even churches—is overrun with depravity. Yet we as a culture pat ourselves on the back and congratulate ourselves for being tolerant of all the depravity that goes on around us. *God has set a standard.* Wickedness and depravity will be punished.

Hosea 9:9 says, "The things my people do are as depraved as what they did in Gibeah long ago. God will not forget. He will surely punish them for their sins" (NLT).

I do not like punishment; never did. Our culture is at a place of decision—continue to accept the depravity that surrounds us, or take up the challenge of change, repent of our wickedness, and turn toward righteousness. I'm running hard after righteousness.

October 22

High-Quality Tools

2 Timothy 2:15

In this age of technology, we would like to believe that things are put together with exact and tested tolerance. We have ability to build tools and equipment that will last forever but often choose to build lesser-quality goods because of cost and a desire to resell an item in a shorter amount of time. I can buy Phillips screw bits for my impact driver relatively cheap, but they only last for a few screws. If I spend money to buy higher-priced bits, they last a lot longer. There is something to be said for longevity and the cost that is often associated with that.

I am probably considered a long-time Christian, as I have been serving the Lord since childhood. At my age, that makes it a long time. I believe that I do have longevity as a Christian. I might be getting older, but the "bit" is still good. I believe that God has invested in me as an individual. And it was not a small or cheap investment. I am someone of value and worth. God spent significant resources in redeeming my life and making me who I am today. I'm glad I'm still in God's toolbox.

October 23

A Spiritual Experience

Ephesians 4:20–24

I heard many references to a recent moon eclipse as being a "spiritual experience," and I do trust that the people were feeling the presence of a holy God who created the event to unfold before us. Deep within the heart and soul of everyone lies a desire to have a spiritual experience, but I also believe that the enemy of our souls wants to fill that desire with many things that seem to satisfy but only last for the moment. The total eclipse, if you were in an area of totality, lasted only a couple of minutes. For me, it was a wonderful experience of God's abilities put on display. But as for its being a spiritual experience, yesterday's eclipse was greatly overshadowed by the experience of sin cleansed from my life and by knowing that the God of creation has taken up residence in my heart, has taken control of my life, and is now steering my course, even to the point that it might block the impact of sin that is focused upon this earth.

If you have never had this spiritual experience, then I highly recommend it. It far surpasses what you experienced in watching the eclipse. And that spiritual experience can continue for the rest of your life. Yep, far better than a two-minute total eclipse.

Experience God the Father, Jesus Christ, the Son of God, and the living Holy Spirit of God in your life today and every day. Now that is a spiritual experience you will not soon forget.

October 24

Upgrading My Experience

Lamentations 3:21–24

Experiencing God in my life is an ever-changing, moment-by-moment experience. It is true that God is "never" changing, but you and I can never exhaust all the experiences God has planned for each one of us. If you think that experiencing God is just a weekly routine of church attendance and a prayer or two during the week, you are missing out—and missing out *big time*. Just as God's mercies are new every morning, so our God experiences are new as well. Yes, some of those experiences take you through trials and sometimes even grief, but God tells us that he will never leave us or forsake us and that he will hold our hands and even carry us when we are in need.

If your God experience is lacking, then I encourage you to join me in church tomorrow. A new beginning, a fresh start, a spiritual boost, an inspiring God-appointed experience awaits you when you attend churches that preach and teach the full gospel of Jesus Christ. A new God experience for each one there. God's promise from His Word is that He will be there, and I have experienced God enough to know that it will be a great experience as God shows up with His new mercies and new experiences.

Come and see that the Lord our God is *good*. A great experience, a God experience, awaits you. Attend a church where God is free to pour out a new and fresh experience for you.

Hill City First Assembly of God
206 N. Middle, Hill City
9:30 Sunday school
10:45 worship

This is my home church, and I invite you to come. I look forward to seeing you there.

October 25

The Assembly

Hebrews 10:25

I'm going to church today, both this morning for Sunday school and worship service and again this evening for the evangelistic service at six o'clock. I go because I want to go, not because I must go. I'm not teaching, preaching, or leading worship, and if I wasn't there, someone else could surely welcome folks and take up the offering. I'm going to church for the following reasons:

1. I was raised going to church for every service. It's a great habit to have.
2. God commands in His Word to "forsake not the gathering of ourselves together."
3. God promises to meet with those gathered there each time we meet.
4. I know the music and worship will be lively but sincere, providing an atmosphere to collectively worship God in His house.
5. I also know that the truth of God's Word will be taught, preached and proclaimed by Holy Spirit–anointed teachers, worship leaders, and our pastors.

6. Many of my closest friends will be there, helping all of us to draw closer to God and one another in unity.
7. Church, God's house, is where God's healing power flows freely; where miracles take place; where lives are restored; where those with mental anguish are set free; where those with life-controlling habits, thoughts, and vices are set free in Jesus's name; and where the captive are set free. I desire to witness these events as they happen and not just hear about it.
8. God will often speak directly to us through the gifts of the Holy Spirit, including messages in tongues and interpretation, word of knowledge, and word of wisdom.
9. I will witness the saving power of Jesus Christ as the Holy Spirit draws unbelievers into a tight relationship with God.
10. I go to church not because of who I am but because of who He is, yesterday, today, tomorrow, and forever—God the Father, Jesus Christ the Son, and the Holy Spirit. He is worthy of my worship and my attendance in church every service.

Just do it. Just go to church—now.

October 26

Routine Maintenance

Hebrews 4:12

If you use a tool a lot, you soon notice that it needs help in maintaining its usability. Our knife drawer at home has an array of very nice knives that are used in the kitchen, but after being used for some time, they lose their edge and sharpness. They are very good knives but are not doing the job well that they were designed for. Some maintenance is needed. We also have a nice butcher's steel, and with a few strokes on the steel, those knives become as sharp as new, perhaps even sharper.

In my walk with God, there are times when maintenance is needed. I have been created with ability and productivity, but sometimes I just need a little sharpening. The "steel" of God's Word, God's Spirit, and God's hand upon my life does just that, and so often am I better than before because of the maintenance. I may not be the sharpest knife in the drawer, but I have been created as high quality, and with some sharpening from God's steel, I am usable.

Lord God Almighty, allow this "knife" to be used again and again, and maintain me as needed.

October 27

Change of Plans

Isaiah 43:18–19

My perspective today is what this day brings, not what might have been. Life occasionally takes a turn, sometimes a very sharp turn. Sometimes I have wonderful plans in place—plans that I believe God would approve of, plans that I have prepared for—and perhaps I'm even in the middle of those plans when there is sudden change. Too often, we humans are prone to dwelling on what could have been because of all the planning and work put into what we are doing, and when change is forced upon us, we still want to dwell on the what-could-have-been.

Change, even huge change that catches us unexpectedly, was never a surprise to God, to whom I have given my life. Perhaps it's too simple to really grasp, but I can take my surprise change and give it to my God, who was not surprised, and just simply ask, "What are we (God and I) going to do now?" God is instantaneous, while my human flesh makes me a bit slower.

God, if you desire that my plans change today, I do want to be in Your will. Help me to recognize more quickly and respond wholly to where You are taking me.

Change in plans? God knew, and He has a great new plan. Let's focus on the what-will-be, not on the what-might-have-been.

October 28

Holy Spirit Outpouring

Joel 2:1–32

God is up to something. That shouldn't be a surprise because God has been up to something for the whole of eternity. As humans, we may grasp the idea of God's creating the heavens and the earth as kind of a starting point—for some reason, we humans just need a starting point. But do you ever wonder what God was doing during the eons of time before the creation of this world? I think it is probable that God had other "projects" going on before the heavens and earth were created, and perhaps He has other ongoing projects occurring simultaneously with this project we are familiar with.

So, for the past five thousand years or so, God has done some amazing things. Creation; creation of man and woman; worldwide flood; humanity divided into different language-speaking groups; crossing of the Red Sea on dry ground; birth of God's Son as a human being; miracles, signs, and wonders; great outpouring of God's Holy Spirit; great awakening; mighty revivals—the list could go on. What is God about to do in the heartland of the United States? Many prophetic messages, words of knowledge, messages in tongues, and interpretations give a clear message that God is about bring a great and mighty move toward God as never seen before. Just as a change in human behavior must start with a change of heart, so a great change to desire the things of God will start in the heartland.

As the heart of America changes to go hard after God, the rest of this nation will be impacted to go hard after God. I don't know the time frame, but I know that we are in the season. Prepare yourself. God is up to something, and it is world-changing big! I'm glad I live in the heartland.

October 29

Alexa, Can I Communicate with God?

Hebrews 4:12–16

I had the privilege of working yesterday with Alexa, who is employed by my company. She is very smart, has many skills, is friendly, and has a pleasant voice. She has great ability to retrieve data seemingly from thin air and is willing to ask questions and formulate responses that are appropriate. Alexa is not a real human being, though she has a voice and an identity. Alexa is artificial-intelligence technology that has been developed to do the many things she can do—certainly a remarkable combination of technology. Humans have been able to do tremendous things with technology the last thirty years, and I enjoy using many of those inventions. As amazing as human technology is, the human being still is even more amazing. When you consider the wonder of God's "technology," you must be amazed and be in jaw-dropping awe.

You and I are true wonders of technology. And to think that the God of this universe created us with an ability to communicate with Him. You and I are not artificial, and our intelligence is not artificial either. God has given us sound minds that can do much good. Let God give you wisdom and power to live your life today.

He alone is my source and strength.

October 30

Abundantly Exceeding Expectations

Ephesians 3:20–21

Exceedingly and *abundantly* are two words that capture my attention in scripture. Occurring forty times in God's Word, the word *exceedingly* portrays a clear picture of something far beyond expectation or comprehension. *Abundantly* occurs thirty-two times and indicates a supply that is more than just enough. When the words exceedingly and abundantly occur together, it brings into play a compounding and multiplication factor that is beyond our understanding.

When God's Word declares that God is able to do exceedingly and abundantly far more than what we can ask or think, the reality is that the possibilities are endless, the miracles are countless, and the results are boundless. Far too often, I find myself limiting God to my finite ways and understanding. It is time that we who serve God let our faith swell to a point of unfathomable greatness and allow God to do the *exceedingly* and *abundantly* that He so much wants to do.

Lord God Almighty, help me to push aside doubt and fear, and let giant faith take its place in my life today. Exceedingly and abundantly—it's for the kingdom of God today.

October 31

Getting to the Bottom of This

Proverbs 25:2

The length of life that I have lived has given me a lot of experience and perhaps even some wisdom. I have been in my line of work for over thirty years, and my experience there would perhaps qualify me as an expert, at least in the opinion of some with whom I work. I have learned much while doing my job. Recently, I was given a task to complete that called upon all this experience that I have, as well as my seeking advice and help from others within this industry. The task has proven extremely challenging and is not yet completed. Frustration could certainly become a powerful influence, but it does not solve the problem.

The writer of Proverbs reveals to us, "The honor of kings is to search out a matter". (Proverbs 25:2 AKJV) That is where I am at with this task. I'm not sure that *delight* is a word that best describes my attitude, but I certainly know that I will be delighted when we have come to the end of the matter, and the task is completed. God's promise in these situations is that if we lack wisdom, all we must do is ask, and He will give to us the wisdom needed to find the answer. Man's wisdom is insufficient, especially in this matter, but God is *all-knowing*. And He knows what the answer is. My thinking that my unsolved task is big or small does not matter. I serve a *big* God who delights in helping with even the smallest of problems.

God Almighty, I look to You for the wisdom to find the answer. You are able—more than able—to do exceedingly and abundantly more than we can ask or even think. That's awesome! I wait expectantly for your help.

2018 update—God gave us an answer to what we sought. It was a long and tedious process, involving numerous tests and the involvement of several scientists. Thank you, almighty God, Creator of all, for giving us the long-awaited answer.

November 1

Godliness

Hebrews 13:5–7

As we gather today in thousands of churches across America, it is vital that we pray for this nation and for the election that takes place on Tuesday. We do not pray that our favorite candidate wins but that God would intervene in the hearts of individuals and direct our steps and our votes. We pray that the weapons that are formed against us by the enemy of our souls would not prosper and that they would be revealed for what they are.

We pray for an awakening of Christians to stand up and be counted for righteousness, holiness, and godliness. We pray that those who oppose righteousness, holiness, and godliness would be met by a loving God who would open their eyes from the blindness that they are trapped in. We pray for a powerful move of a holy God to sweep across this nation in such manner that sin, degradation, and immorality are cast out, and eternal life is accepted by those who are set free. We pray for a revitalization of Christian zeal that becomes a passion in the lives of millions across this land. We pray in repentance for our lackluster attempt to be followers of the one, true, living God, the only God who can set captives free and redeem us from our sin. We pray that in all that we do, even our voting on Tuesday, God would be glorified. Amen.

November 2

Longevity

Psalm 1:1–3

In the alfalfa seed industry where I work, a common questions I get about the varieties that I represent is, "What is the persistence?" That means, *How long can I expect the alfalfa stand to last?* Persistence in the Christian life is also important. I believe that God's salvation through Jesus Christ is a constant and will remain until God allows Jesus to take the church out of this world, but I also believe that God is looking for persistence and longevity in the lives of those who accept His salvation.

As Christians, we are to bear fruit, and that takes time and persistence. God's Word refers to being "like a tree planted by the water," receiving water, nutrients, and care for a long-lasting relationship with God. Yes, there may be storms, harsh winters, and so on, but stay rooted, and feed on the Word of God. Let's all be persistent in our relationship with God through Jesus Christ. My desire is to remain persistent until He comes for me.

November 3

Only a Boy

1 Samuel 16:1–13

One of my favorite Bible stories is the story of David and Goliath. Growing up, I was one of the smaller kids in my class and was never looked upon as anyone of importance. My favorite song of this story is, "Only a boy named David." In the story, nothing is said about the power of God coming upon David, only an inspiration put in David's heart and mind to do something that involved his skill and ability. Growing up, I identified with David—not that I was a giant-slayer but only a boy.

There was nothing special about David. He was the youngest boy of his family. He was a shepherd boy, whose position was usually looked upon as being a "lowly shepherd." But God chose to use David, only a boy. When I look back upon my life and see how God has chosen me, only a boy, to do what He has placed in my heart and mind, with the skills and abilities that God has helped me develop, I am simply amazed. I'm only a boy. Yet God has used, is using, and will use me.

You may think you are nobody special and the skills and abilities you have developed in life are not anything great. Perhaps David thought from time to time, *Why am I out here watching sheep when everyone else is off doing something more exciting?* And as he was thinking those thoughts, he was practicing sharpshooting with his slingshot. I have no idea how many practice shots David made with his slingshot, but I suspect it was thousands, perhaps tens of thousands, and his fame came with just one shot.

Practice the skills and abilities that God has given you, even if you are an older person like me. God has a plan to use those skills and abilities. Make the first shot count. I'm only a boy, and I am still practicing well into my seventh decade of life. God's plan involves both me and you. It may just be that a giant needs slaying.

November 4

Knocking on the Door

Revelation 3:20

It took 120 years to prepare for a promised flood that would completely destroy humankind, unless they were saved by being on the ark—120 years, and nobody listened. Nobody! That is, nobody outside of Noah and his immediate family—eight humans, total, who were saved from destruction. Everyone else—*everyone*—was destroyed because of their wickedness.

For those who are convinced that God would never pronounce a complete judgment upon humankind because God is a good God, I beg to differ. It won't be a flood, because of God's promise signed by a rainbow, but God's Word is absolutely clear that those who are not saved by the blood of Jesus Christ will be judged and found guilty, just as guilty as those who lost their lives in the flood in Noah's day, and will spend eternity in hell. The Word of God tells us that the last thing that happens to this earth will be that it and everything that inhabits it, including those humans who have not been taken away in the rapture of the church (those who are not saved), will be destroyed by fire.

I believe this will be an all-consuming fire that will cleanse the earth. I say that because God is referred to in His Word as "an All-Consuming Fire." Either way, dead or alive, I want to be among that number who are saved. I am sure of my salvation through Jesus Christ. I want you to be sure as well. The door is open; come on in. It's not too late.

Make sure you are among those who are saved. It's simple. Acknowledge to God that you are a sinner and that you need God's free gift of salvation. Ask Jesus Christ, the Son of God, to cleanse your heart of sin, and come into your heart to live there. Then thank Him for doing so. After you have done that, find a good Bible-teaching and Bible-believing church, and join other Christians in rejoicing over your salvation. Do it now, before it is too late!

November 5

Signs of the End

2 Timothy 3:1-5

A lot of information has been shared regarding the eclipses and the path that both will take across the United States in 2017, as well as the alignment of the stars in a formation believed to be indicated in God's Word regarding last days. I am not an expert, but I know that God's Word declares that the sun, moon, and stars were created, in part, to be "signs in the heavens." I believe that God is desiring to get man's attention at least one final time before the end of the age, and I do believe that we are living in the last days of this age.

Simply, I believe that the heavens' signs and wonders declare the soon coming of Jesus Christ in the clouds of glory to take the true church of Jesus Christ and the presence of the Son of God out of this world. That event will take place in a moment, in a twinkling of an eye—instantaneous and earth-shaking. It could happen before you finish reading this. It could happen today, or before the eclipse on Monday, or before the forty days that occur after the eclipse, leading to Yom Kipper. I'm ready. I'm ready for a great awakening or the Lord's coming. Either one—I am ready!

November 6

The Beginning

Genesis 1:1-26

If you have doubts about the existence of God, who was the Author and Creator of everything that we know to be in existence today and so much more that we don't know, then I invite you to consider the signs of the heavens that are upcoming. At a minimum, some five thousand years ago at the time of creation, God created the heavens and the earth. In the heavens, God created the sun, moon, and stars, and God set their path. At creation, God knew the path that the moon would take on August 21, 2017, to cause a full eclipse across a land yet not formed, and He also knew exactly where the stars that He had thrown into space would be in 2017–18, to be signs to the inhabitants of earth. I live within a two-hour drive of where the total eclipse will occur, and I may drive there, just to say that I experienced it.

But there's this one thing: Lord God Almighty, Creator of the heavens, sun, moon, stars, and earth, help us to not get so caught up in seeking the signs of Your return that we forget to keep a constant watch for Your Son, Jesus's, return. The signs are pointing to that great event. I don't want to be caught seeking signs and not seeking Jesus's return. Even so, come, Lord Jesus.

November 7

God's Great Abilities

1 Chronicles 29:11

God's abilities are far beyond human imagination and thinking. Too often we want to limit God with our severely limited human thinking. As I grow older, I find myself thinking more and more about what God really wants to do, when in fact I am limiting Him with what I allow Him to do. Can I just step into the bigness of God's plan and be involved in the "beyond what we can imagine or even think"? Absolutely, but first I must take the advice found in God's Word and die to self. When the flesh is dead and buried, then the greatness of God can flourish. Let God's greatness flourish. I desire to step aside for that. Let's just see what God can do. I'm ready to once again be amazed by God.

A Restless World

Matthew 6:34

Today (in 2017), the total eclipse will occur across the United States. What follows in the hours, days, and weeks after the eclipse is in God's control. It is obvious that humankind and nature are restless going into this time frame. If we, as humans, allow the restlessness to cause us to seek after God, then I believe a great move of God, unlike anything in history, awaits us. If we allow our restlessness to push us into more hate and sin against one another and God, then I believe we stand before the judgment of a righteous and holy God. I believe we are at a precipice, tottering on the brink of falling into God's judgment. Our only hope is God's mercy, extended to us to allow repentance to take place.

Father in heaven, I join with countless others in repenting of our sins as a nation. We have quit honoring You on the Sabbath. We have made the murder of innocent babies conceived in your image and in your presence the law of our land for many years. We have contrived every evil to better ourselves over our neighbor, stealing what our neighbor has and making ourselves rich by doing so. We have sinned—greatly sinned—against You, O Lord, and I, along with others, repent and ask forgiveness of our sins. We seek a mighty move of God that the Holy Spirit would uncover, reveal, and make known the deep wickedness that prevails in our world and that a wave, many waves, of repentance would flood our land.

Lord God Almighty, let Your Holy Spirit move in power, and let all humankind be drawn to Jesus as our Savior. Amen.

Our prayers and voices joined together are a powerful tool that moves the heart and hand of Almighty God.

November 9

Spiritual Contrast

Romans 8:5–11

Contrast adds interesting highlights to our lives. Contrast makes what we see with our physical eyes clearer and sharper and can be as obvious as night and day or black and white. There are also contrasts between our heavenly Father and the enemy of our souls, Satan. God desires to do good to each of us; Satan desires to destroy us. God gives good gifts to us; Satan's gifts are vices and imprisonment. God, through Jesus Christ, provides salvation; Satan's only offer is eternal damnation. God's Holy Spirit comes alongside as a helper and comforter; Satan gives out turmoil and loneliness. God and Satan—what a contrast, and yet so many today are blinded by Satan and can't see the goodness of God.

Lord God Almighty, help me to show the goodness of God to everyone I encounter.

November 10

Spiritual Check

Colossians 3:1–17

Dental and physical checkups are a routine in our lifestyles today. Maintaining a healthy body is important, though I think the doctors want to see me more often than I really need to see them. Physical maintenance is important for staying healthy as I get older, and the doctors lend their expertise in keeping me healthy.

It's important to maintain a healthy spiritual life as well. A mature Christian having a mature faith is an honorable attribute. As I grow older, if I just sat and did nothing in my physical life, my body would deteriorate, losing its strength, stamina, and mental ability. Exercise and activity help to maintain a physical body so that it can still be strong and have stamina and a sharp mind.

In our spiritual lives, we must also stay active. I think God desires each of to be active in our walk before Him until He calls us home. I desire to hear from God each day and set about doing what He has called me to do. *Doing*—it's an activity that's important for my Christian walk. *Doing* helps maintain my spiritual being.

November 11

Defending Freedom

Isaiah 1:17

Though I did not serve in the military, I have a deep gratitude for those who have served and are now serving. From the time that men chose to take up arms and defend their right to create a new nation that honored God and acknowledged His sovereignty over this new nation, until today, where men and women are defending human rights and protecting our freedom, men and women have stepped into the role of being protectors and defenders of freedom. A thank-you is obviously not enough to express the gratitude this nation must have for those who are serving or have served. This nation and I are grateful. We can have a peaceful transition of leadership because of those who have served and those serving today. I am grateful. God has blessed us with a willing group of military personnel who willingly do what they are called to do. We make our nation great again, in part, because we will fully support our military. God bless America.

Rev. Franklin Graham says it best—it is time to rise up and go forward for the army of the Lord.

November 12

In a Tough Place

Isaiah 41:10

Sometimes we find ourselves in a bad situation or difficult position, caused by our own actions, but at other times, it's simply by the work and action of the enemy of our souls. The apostle Paul found himself in prison many different times, not because he deserved it but because Satan, the enemy of our souls, desired to stop the spread of the gospel message.

God wants you to know that He has not forgotten you or overlooked you; rather, He has chosen to be with you with every step as you go through whatever you are in right now. Like Paul, if you are in prison, God is with you every moment of every day. If life has thrown you down and has walked or even stomped on you, know that Jesus is lying there beside you and has more than enough strength to pick you up, dust you off, and continue your walk with Him. If you're down today, let Jesus hug your neck and draw you close.

If you live close enough to LaDonna and me, find us or let us know. We've got a hug for you as well. God has an excellent record of restoration. Let Him restore you today.

November 13

Chain Breaker

Mark 5:1–43

Christian rock artist Zach Williams wrote these words for us to contemplate. (By the way, it's a great song that's been sung by several different groups.)

If you've got pain,
He's a pain taker.
If you feel lost,
He's a way maker.
If you need freedom or saving,
He's a prison-shaking Savior.
If you've got chains,
He's a chain breaker.

God is in the business of breaking chains that bind us. You have not experienced real freedom until your chains have been broken, and you have been set free. You only need to ask God to break your chains, and in His great love, God will set you free. God is a chain breaker.

November 14

Boldness—A Godly Characteristic

Ephesians 3:12

Bold—it's a term we apply to coffee, print, moves, courage, and life. By nature, I am not a bold person. I'll wait to see if the other vehicle will make it through the mudhole before I try. I'll wait to hear how good something is before I buy it. One of the characteristics that God gives today to those who are filled with His Holy Spirit is boldness. The men and women who came out of the upper room on the day of Pentecost were filled with boldness beyond belief. They came from hiding behind closed doors to boldly proclaiming the gospel of Jesus Christ. As I look at our culture and world today, I see a huge need for *boldness*, not man-made but God-inspired and God-applied. Lord God Almighty, fill your people with Your Holy Spirit, and place *boldness* into our lives for today's needs.

Witnessing—It's Easier than You Think

1 Peter 3:15; Colossians 4:6

Being a "witness" for Jesus brings many thoughts to mind, including going into our community and knocking on doors of people we don't know (or don't know very well). That activity puts almost everyone in panic mode and creates an intense desire to not participate—me included. While God does call and provide a passion to some to be involved in this type of activity, I believe that for many, our calling to share the gospel is somewhat different. The term *witness* carries with it a meaning of seeing or experiencing something that needs to be shared. A witness to a crime must tell his or her story to the police to verify what happened. An expert witness can explain how something works accurately in the way it was designed, or it will be subject to failure because of defects.

As Christians, those to whom God has given His glorious salvation, we have been witness to what God has done in our lives. The stories are many and varied in each of our lives, but each of us has witnessed God's grace, love, and mercy. The question I ask myself is this: Have I told my stories and shared what I have witnessed with all my family and friends? Sharing our individual stories with our family and friends is not difficult. It can start with a statement like this: "I want to tell you my story." All of us like stories, and when they are personal, they have even deeper meaning. Let's share what we have witnessed. Our stories of what we have seen God do—our *witness*—can change the lives of those we call family and friends.

November 16

Be Generous with Patience

Romans 15:5

Generosity comes in many forms. Those who have driven on Highway 76 through Branson, Missouri, during peak traffic flow know how slow traffic moves and how many cars want to join the parade. Generosity is shown by thousands during the day as they stop long enough to allow another vehicle to cross over or pull in front of them, or as they pull out of a parking lot, allowing alternating vehicles to exit from two or more lines. All of this is done without traffic control or police direction. It is the generosity of those who are willing to allow the other to go first that makes traffic flow smoothly—slow but smoothly.

Many times, generosity does not cost money, only time and a little patience. Often my patience is short, especially with family members. I guess if I can be patient with traffic in Branson, I can be patient in other places and with other family members. Generous patience—I'm still learning, even at my age. I'm learning how to tap the horn only lightly. Patience—it's not that the rest of the world needs more; it's that I need to use it more.

November 17

Come Before God with Boldness

Hebrews 4:16

God knew beforehand every need I have ever faced or will face in the future. Simply put, He knew before I knew. Sometimes, as we live life, we know that we have needs but remain silent toward God, knowing that He already knows. God's Word, though, shares this concept: we are to boldly come before the throne of grace and present our needs.

There is just something awe-inspiring about putting words to our thoughts and expressing them to God Almighty through Jesus Christ. Think of it this way: Who is the most important or prominent individual with whom you have ever had a conversation? What did you say to that person? In looking back, did you think "I should have said ..." or "I should have asked this question"? Perhaps it was a once-in-a-lifetime opportunity.

But Almighty God, the creator of all that we know and so much more, invites us to come into His presence and ask boldly for His intervention into our lives to meet our needs. Yes, the one to whom every world leader, king, and ruler will bow down invites you to talk with Him—and not just talk but to ask for His help. And the amazing thing is that it's not just a once-in-a-lifetime deal. We can come back time after time, again and again.

As you do so, you will discover that the closeness and relationship that you are building allows for easy conversation and ease of asking God for His help. God's Word also proclaims this fact: God can do exceedingly more than we can ask or even think. Many today are thinking wonderful thoughts of what God can do. It's now time to boldly *ask*. God is available for you to ask right now.

November 18

Most Unlikely

1 Corinthians 1:24–31

God is not a respecter of persons. As Christians, we have heard that statement proclaimed many times when someone is encouraging involvement in the kingdom of God and being used of God to build the kingdom. The leader chosen by God to bring Israel out of the slavery of Egypt had a speech impediment—he stuttered—and others most likely often made fun of him for this disability, yet God chose him to be the nation's leader. Paul the apostle was a murderer, focused on destroying the Christian faith and movement, yet God called him to be an evangelist. Peter, a devout Jew who would have nothing to do with "unclean" things, including gentiles, was called of God to minister to the unclean.

In today's world, God is still calling unlikely individuals to build the kingdom of God. I am one of those unlikely folks. I cannot tell you why God chose me to do what I do, but He did anyway, and I marvel at how God uses me. I am discovering that God doesn't just select a small percentage. Rather, God chooses whom He chooses to use by the multitudes. If you are reading this, there is a high likelihood that God has chosen you to help build His kingdom. My advice: prepare to be amazed. God is at work, and for Him, nothing is impossible.

November 19

It Is Finished

John 19:28–30

It is finished. The painting project is done. What could have taken just a short time was interrupted by life, but tenacity and endurance won out, and it is finished. Jesus spoke those same words as He gasped His last breath before dying upon the cross. The plan that had been laid out since before creation had finally been completed. The age of God's laws being difficult to keep was now replaced by mercy and grace. God's required blood covering for sin was now complete, with the final sacrifice of His only Son, Jesus Christ. All that is required for atonement of my sin was hanging from that cross, with Jesus's blood dripping to the ground.

When I ask Jesus into my heart and life, He covers me with His blood. I become His child, and my name is written in the Lamb's book of life. I have not been made perfect, but because of the blood covering, I have been made righteous. As a New Testament believer, I'll receive that identification over an Old Testament lawbreaker any time—made righteous.

Redeeming God, thank you for my salvation. The work was finished on the cross. All I must do is receive it, and I receive it again today.

November 20

Worry—Don't

Philippians 4:4–9

No matter where you look, you can see that biblical end-time prophecies are being fulfilled all around us. Fires in the western United States placed a lot of smoke and haze in the air in early September 2017. Last night as the sun set, the smoke and haze caused the sun to take on a red-globe appearance, blotting out its brilliance. One can only imagine what it would be like if a gigantic volcanic eruption took place upon this earth, spewing trillions of tons of ash into the atmosphere.

I can certainly get a concept of the sun's being blotted out and the catastrophic results that would occur. But I do not worry about such things that might possibly happen. God's Word says this about worry: How can my worry change what is going to occur in the future? Simply put, worry only upsets our emotional balance and causes us to be consumed by our fears. The Word of God encourages us to be consumed not of fear but of love.

Catastrophic events are bound to happen in our lifetimes, but worry will not change a thing as to whether it happens or when it happens. Love, though, can be bestowed at any time under any circumstance, and when we love, our emotions are soothed, healed, and strengthened.

If you have fears in your life, here is God's remedy: Love casteth out all fear. Please understand that in God's Word, *all* has only one meaning—nothing or no one left out. Let love fill your life and watch the fear depart.

November 21

The Presence of God

Psalm 16:7–11

It is one of those wonderful, crisp fall mornings that we experience in our four-seasons part of the world—just the slightest of breezes and the sun burning off the haze of humidity hanging in the air. Nature mirrors the presence of God in our lives and our world. Let His sweet presence encompass your life today.

The day will change as it progresses, but God's sweet presence will continue and take you into tomorrow, the Lord's day. See you in church tomorrow for another great encounter with God and friends.

November 22

Gathering Empty Vessels

2 Kings 4:1–7

I want to share what God has quickened in my spirit and perhaps can be considered a word of knowledge or a prophetic word given by God's Holy Spirit. Second Kings 4 contains the story of the prophet Elisha, who had asked for and received a double portion of the Spirit of God that had rested upon his mentor, Elijah. Elisha received a visit from a widow who owed a great debt to creditors, and she asked him to help. When he asked what she had in the house, her reply was nothing, "save a pot of oil."

Elisha told her, "Go, borrow Thee vessels abroad of all thy neighbors, even empty vessels; borrow not a few." (2 Kings 4:3 AKJV) The widow was instructed to shut the door of her house, and then she and her sons were to pour out the oil from her pot into all the vessels, and "she poured out." When all the vessels were full, she asked her sons to bring more, and their reply was, "There is not a vessel more. And the oil stayed."

God says to His church today to bring into His sanctuary all the "vessels" (people), even those who are empty and even chipped or cracked and in need of repair. God is getting ready to pour out the oil of His Holy Spirit, not on just a few but upon and in all those who have been gathered together. The flow of the Holy Spirit will not stop until all the vessels are filled to overflowing. Like in the story of 2 Kings 4, our instructions are to bring in every vessel (person) we can find—and not just a few.

God is quickening His timetable as the whole earth anticipates His return. We must act quickly and decisively, as God is ready to do what He says He will do. Empty, damaged, even broken vessels (individuals)—you are welcome in my church. God is getting ready to pour into your life His Holy Spirit in quantities you cannot fully contain, and others need to be there to catch the overflow.

Jesus's words to us as He went back to heaven to be with His Father was that all the things we watched Him do, we would be able to do and even more, perhaps a double portion, because of the Holy Spirit being poured out upon and into you and me.

Lord God Almighty, I desire a double portion of Your Holy Spirit upon my life. Let Your Holy Spirit flow into every life.

November 23

Wallowing in the Muck and Mire

2 Peter 2:17–22

We live in a world that seems to thrive on fake news, false accusations, and outright lies about others. Truth has been set aside so that we can wallow in the muck and mire of falsehood. It reminds me of pigs wallowing in a hog wallow. Pigs are raised in a dirt-floor penned environment, and it doesn't take long for the pigs to root out a good size hole to lie down in. When the hole fills with water from rainfall or overfill from the water trough, they love to just lie in the muck and mire of the dirt, feces, and everything else that finds its way in there.

In the summertime they will lie in that for hours, with only their eyes and nose sticking out. And the smell is bad beyond explanation. Usually there is a dry and somewhat clean area in the same pen, but they delight in spending their time in the wallow. As a society and culture, we are encapsulated with the muck and mire of what we allow to surrounded us. I think that not even our noses remain above the wallow.

It is time that we pull ourselves out of the wallow and demand truth. God's Word promises that truth will set us free. If this is true—and it is—that means that we are bound up when we accept fake news, falsehoods, and lies into our lives. Freedom—it's found in the truth.

November 24

Doing What's Right

James 4:17

Many people stand on the brink of a decision, knowing what is right, but they are pulled toward making the wrong decision. Not quickly making the right decision allows for the persuasion of a wrong or poor choice to tug at our heart. Make the right decision quickly and then stand firm with it.

God's Word shares this: "To Him that knoweth to do good and does it not, to Him it is sin" (James 4:17).

Here's a piece of advice for today and for future reference: when you know what the right choice is, make that your choice, and make it quickly. Stewing and fretting only gives opportunity for the wrong decision to be made. Once the right choice is made, go hard after it, and forget the enticement of the wrong decision.

November 25

Proven and Shareable

Titus 2:1–10

Research is important to the industry I am in. Knowing the capability, persistence, and inadequacies of the products that I represent is important to how I place them with customers, who rely upon me for true and accurate information as to variety placement. As I approach being an "older" Christian (at least in the eyes of some, especially my grandkids, I am "old"), I find more and more that younger and inexperienced Christians look to me for advice and wisdom. I can share from a life of experience serving God. The testing I have gone through has proven, time and again, the value and truth of God's holy Word and the promises that He gives uniquely to me and to all who seek after Him.

Just as I can say with confidence to an alfalfa grower that a specific variety will do very well for him, and I give advice on its care and management, so my life and testing can provide insight and wisdom to others. That is true for all Christians who have maturity and have been tested in life. Perfect? Uh, no, not yet, but tried and tested, I can testify to God's great ability and power. My life has been a research project for the Lord Jesus Christ, and I can confidently share with you that serving God will work for you and will be the best fit in your life—far better than anything else you can plant in your life. I know—because I am one of the research projects that proves it.

November 26

Thanksgiving Harvest

Matthew 9:35–38

Happy Thanksgiving, everyone. I am thankful for men and women who were willing to leave family, home, and everything else and come to America. Their purpose was to establish a new world that would allow them to openly worship the true living God without oppression. This movement took great effort and cost a significant number of lives, but as that group of Pilgrims sat down to the first Thanksgiving dinner, they gave thanks to the living God for His goodness and His provision. I am thankful that today I perceive a similar spirit of seeking God and His righteousness stirred up in this world and its cultures today.

There isn't a new world to move to and begin again, but *this* world is ripe for a spiritual harvest that is beyond imagination. Pray ye that the Lord of the harvest would send forth workers into the field. I am thankful for the harvest that awaits in abundance. I am thankful that men and women of all walks of life are feeling and hearing the call of God to enter the harvest field. I am thankful that the spirit of worshiping the one true God is rising among us in vast numbers today.

November 27

Spiritual Maintenance

Psalm 51:10

It is time to do some maintenance on my company-provided truck. Today, an oil change and a change-out of front wheel bearings will be done. These are routine things that occur periodically and must be done to keep the vehicle running properly. There are things that should occur in our Christian walk that will maintain our Christian faith, including daily prayer, Bible reading, and going to church at least once a week.

My vehicle comes with a manual that indicates an oil change should occur after a certain number of miles, more often if it operates in dirty conditions. That is true of our prayers, Bible reading, and church attendance. This ol' world that we live in is full of muck and mire, and sometimes it splashes on us. Our manual, God's Word, tells us that when that happens, we need more of God—more maintenance, not less. If life has been tough on you, and the muck and mire have accumulated in your life, go to God, His Word, and His house more than usual, and allow God to give you the maintenance you need.

Because I Said So

2 Timothy 3:10–17

Why do I need to do that? That is probably one of the questions we all ask the most in life. If you have kids or grandchildren, then I know you have been hit with this question over and over. How do we respond? Sometimes with a detailed explanation that takes longer to deliver than just doing the task, and sometimes with just a short-but-sweet reply: "Because I said so."

I wonder if God gets tired of our asking that question of Him. I love the detailed responses God sometimes gives. But at other times, God simply responds, "Because I told you so."

Another quick question—in these cases, who is the parent? Who has authority? When Grandpa tells the grandchildren it's time to put the toys away, and the children ask the same age-old question—"Why do I need to do that?"—that same thought process follows through because it needs to be done (and I did ask nicely).

"But Grandpa, I'm coming back tomorrow and will play with these toys again."

You see, they don't know that Grandma and Grandpa are having company over later, and we need the toys picked up. It's the same way with God. Sometimes—most of the time—I am not aware of what the future holds, but Father God does, and He sometimes does not offer an explanation. Sometimes, "because I said so" is enough.

November 29

For the Win

1 Corinthians 9:24

Every sport has a goal to achieve as the game is played. Ultimately, the goal is to win by scoring points, making baskets, getting the ball over the net or through the opponent's offense, and so on. Christianity also has a goal—making it to heaven. Losing means going to hell. Making it to heaven is not so much having skill; it's more like having a team member, Jesus Christ, the Son of God, who is perfect and has the skill and ability to win the game for us. My decision of which team I want to be on is simple: I choose Jesus's team. I've read the end of the Book. He wins—with an absolute *victory*!

November 30

Cyberspace—God's Domain

Lamentations 3:21–26

Today is "cyber Monday," and millions will order stuff online and pay billions of dollars in credit card payments. In all the cyber activity of my life, communicating with God, my heavenly Father, and with Jesus, the Son of God, I have never been required to submit a monetary payment to receive wonderful gifts from my heavenly Father, whether for myself or others. Think about it: I join with others in praying for healing to take place in someone's life, and it happens. Didn't cost a penny from a monetary standpoint. I pray for someone who is in a desperate situation, and God responds by changing the situation. It didn't cost a dime from a monetary standpoint. I pray for a need in my own life, and God responds with favor only He could provide, and it didn't cost me a single dollar from a monetary standpoint.

God's Word declares that His mercies are new every day. He will not run out of mercies today or say they're on back order, as some will experience in trying to purchase something online today. We cannot exhaust God's mercies and gifts today. Let me say it again: *we cannot exhaust God's mercies and gifts today.* And there will be a fresh, new supply tomorrow. I enjoy my "cyber" time with God.

December 1

Faster and Faster

Ephesians 5:15–16

As we roll into the last thirty-one days of the year, we are reminded that the clock is ticking. Not slower or faster than previously, but it's *seemingly* faster as things begin to bunch up. Note to self: it's already a steep climb to the end of the year. Pushing something off until later in the year only makes the climb steeper, and I'll need to sprint to the finish.

I believe that the clock is also ticking in biblical end times. Not faster or slower, but as we approach that day, much will need to be accomplished. A great harvest of souls awaits. Only God knows the numbers, but every day that passes by pushes the numbers up even more. I envision a sprint to the finish to accomplish all that God desires to accomplish.

Lord, prepare my heart and life to accomplish what needs done in my own life but even more so in my life in You, to accomplish all that you want in these last days.

December 2

A Question or a Statement

Luke 18:18–30

It's the first week of December, and so it begins. LaDonna asked me if I was going to help bake cookies this week. It really isn't a question, although it was posed as such. It's a statement, letting me know that my help is expected (and needed) to prepare the Christmas cookie orders she has in hand. God's Word also contains questions that are really statements. Who shall be saved? Who shall be a witness for me? Who shall I send? Between work, LaDonna, and God, I have plenty to do this week. Will work for cookies. Taste, and see that the Lord, He is good. Best of two worlds this week.

December 3

Let Compassion Move Us

Mark 6:34

What takes place when those who need God to do something in their lives enter my church? Those needs may range from something small to something way beyond human ability—from the meeting of a financial need to a miracle far exceeding man's involvement. My guess is that even in a small congregation like ours, people will walk through the doors who need healing in their bodies, who need reassurance that someone cares, who need joy restored to their lives, souls, and spirits, and who need the miraculous in their lives and families. Most will enter, knowing their needs but reluctant to verbalize their needs that are so well hidden.

When Jesus walked this earth and encountered those in need (today, those who walked through the door), He had compassion for them and healed them all. Nowhere is it recorded in scripture that Jesus prayed for someone, and they did not receive. Our directive—mine and yours—from God's Word is to be like Jesus. He is the Son of God, God in human flesh, able to do anything and everything beyond thought or description, and we are just mere humans, flesh and bone, with sinful natures. We become like Jesus by letting the Spirit of God, who also has all power, live through our lives.

Our pastor shared in yesterday's morning service that we must empty our lives to make room for the Spirit of God. Then—and only then—will we see God do the miraculous and see those who enter the house of God leave after being changed by the power of God. I desire to see those who come into the house of God with needs, great or small, leave with those needs met by our Lord God Almighty. It's God's desire that they do so, and the key is emptying our lives and allowing God's Holy Spirit to live in us *and* through us.

Jesus's promise is this: If we allow God's Spirit to fill our lives, we—human flesh prone to sin—will see all that Jesus did being done through us, by the power of God, and even more. Lord God, I surrender all. Fill and saturate my life with Your Holy Spirit.

December 4

Forgiveness—A Key to Unlocking a Heavy Weight

Ephesians 4:25–32

Forgiveness—what a beautiful thing when it is extended to you. How many times have I been forgiven in my lifetime? The number is exceedingly great, and I am thankful. Over my lifetime, my parents, wife, family, friends, neighbors, teachers, pastors, employers, and fellow employees have extended forgiveness countless times and far more than I deserve. However, the one who has forgiven me the most is Jesus Christ, the very Son of God. No, it was not a one-time-and-done matter. Jesus has forgiven me innumerable times and continues to forgive when I ask. I bask in this feeling of being forgiven.

But let me turn the tables. Have I forgiven as often or as much as I have received forgiveness? Sadly, probably not. Yet as I examine my extending forgiveness when it is in my control to do so, it is a powerful tool. With my forgiveness, I possess the ability to free someone from the burden of failure and wrongdoing. In so doing, I also receive the benefit of releasing the burden I carry in my life of the wrongdoing.

In this season of giving, I recommend giving the gift of forgiveness, recognizing that God's Word declares it is more blessed to give than to receive. Give the gift of forgiveness this Christmas. For those forgiven, it will be their greatest gift this year.

December 5

Tests and More Tests

2 Corinthians 13:5–6

I never was one who looked forward to tests, and after I was out of school, I thought I was home-free. Then life happened. The tests were real and sometimes intense. Our walk with Jesus is often interspersed with testing. But sometimes we need to test ourselves. Paul the apostle shares this:

> I will give you all the proof you want that Christ speaks through me. Christ is not weak when he deals with you; he is powerful among you. Although he was crucified in weakness, he now lives by the power of God. We, too, are weak, just as Christ was, but when we deal with you, we will be alive with him

> and will have God's power. Examine yourselves to see if your faith is genuine. Test yourselves. Surely you know that Jesus Christ is among you; if not, you have failed the test of genuine faith. As you test yourselves, I hope you will recognize that we have not failed the test of apostolic authority. (2 Corinthians 13:3–6)

I am captured by the last statement: *As you test yourselves, I hope you will recognize that we have not failed the test of apostolic authority.* Like Paul, my hope is that you will recognize that you have the power of God working within you, and while we are weak, He is strong. As Paul proclaims, 'I can do all things through Christ which strengtheneth me" (Philippians 4:13)

Take the self-test indicated above. If you fail, make changes and improvements, and take the test again. I want not only a passing grade but also a star beside my name on this test. Surely, we know that Jesus Christ is among us. Let's test ourselves to be certain.

December 6

Keep On Keeping On

2 Timothy 2:8–13

As Christians, what do we do with signs and wonders that appear all around us? Some of us chase after the latest teaching and prophet utterances, some study God's Word more in depth, some ignore everything, and still others just keep on keeping on. Paul gave this advice, translated into my words, "Keep on keeping on." As a follower of God, I must remain stable and unshakable, like a tree planted beside the water. My faith in God must not waver in the midst of storms. My trust and confidence are in the one who holds me in the palm of His hand.

The signs we are seeing unfold on all sides of humanity have been predicted for an entire dispensation or more. Seeing them unfold in my lifetime is beyond my comprehension, but I choose to remain steadfast. Jesus is coming, and for many, His coming will catch them by surprise, even while they may run after signs and prophets. Jesus is coming soon. I'm ready! Make sure you are too.

December 7

A Day of Infamy

Revelation 16:12–21

It was a calm and beautiful Sunday morning. No one that early morning would have even considered that it would become "a day of infamy." Over seventy-five years have passed, and it is still a day of infamy. December 7, 1941, will forever be remembered as the day that the Japanese attacked Pearl Harbor in the central Pacific. The United States was aggressively pursuing a negotiated peace settlement for the war activity already occurring in Europe. This attack would pull us away from the peace table and usher us into the thick of World War II.

LaDonna and I have stood on the memorial that hovers over the sunken USS *Arizona*. It was a somber moment in our lives as we reviewed what happened that day. In God's provision, the United States, being forced to leave the peace table and enter war, went on to solidly win the war on all fronts, including the Pacific, though many lives were lost.

Japan did sit down at a table of surrender on board the USS *Missouri* and sign papers of surrender on September 2, 1945, after devastating US atomic bomb attacks on the nation of Japan forced them to concede. For those who think that things just happen and coincidences just occur, I will argue that God has His hand on the affairs of man and nations. He will draw nations away from warfare, or He will draw them into warfare at various times. God's Word is very clear that a time is coming when the nations of this world will be drawn into a place of arranging themselves against Israel. It is destined to be a bloody battle, as the Bible says that the blood will run bridle-deep in the valley.

In the end, God wins. The nation of Israel will stand. Israel's enemy's will be defeated in a blood bath that will make previous wars pale in comparison. We stand today at a place of remembrance, but we also stand at a place of looking ahead to what is to come. Even so, come, Lord Jesus.

December 8

Trading My Burden for Yours

Galatians 6:2–3

God's Word tells us to bear one another's burdens.

> Share each other's burdens, and in this way obey the law of Christ. If you think you are too important to help someone, you are only fooling yourself. You are not that important. (Galatians 6:2–3)

Jesus tells us to let Him take the burden because His burden is light and easy compared to mine or yours. Yes, I have burdens that I carry, but when you share yours with me, I can take them on because God does give strength for me to do so. I am human, and sometimes I just don't want others to know what my burden load is or what I am dealing with, so I stay quiet. But I appreciate those who are close enough to me to recognize that I am carrying a heavy burden and are willing to help carry it.

Some will confide in their friends and family about the burden they are carrying. Our responsibility when we hear of these struggles is to help carry the load. There are a multitude of ways to carry one another's burdens, but there is no better place to carry them than to the feet of Jesus. There, we can exchange not only our own heavy burdens, but also the burden we carry for others with what Jesus has. Remember that Jesus said his load is easy, and His burden is light. Remember God's promise to turn our mourning into dancing, and our sorrow into joy. He will do that and more.

Yes, I will help bear your burden, but let me tell you—I'm taking it to the feet of Jesus because I have experienced the lightness of His load. His is much easier to bear.

December 9

Cousins

Mark 1:1–11

Something often gets overlooked when we read the biblical account of the time surrounding the birth of John the Baptist and Jesus. It had been some four hundred years since the people of Israel had heard directly from a prophet of God. I'll say it this way: if something is not real, and there is no substance to it, it will disappear in far less than four hundred years.

But we find in God's Word that at the time Zachariah was serving in the temple, offering incense before the Lord, there was a large crowd waiting outside the temple, worshiping and praising God. God's Word also lets us know that both Mary and Joseph were devout followers of God, along with their families and many others in and around the city of Nazareth. When Jesus was dedicated in Jerusalem on the eighth day after his birth, there were those who had dedicated themselves to a lifetime of fasting and prayer before God, never leaving the temple.

Maybe you haven't heard from God in a while, but that does not make God nonexistent. The reality is that God is every bit as much God as He has ever been, even if we have not heard from Him for a while. Just as history shows that God was up to something big some two thousand years ago, I believe God is up to something even bigger and more profound today.

Meanwhile, I am going to continue to worship and serve Him today because I have experienced Him. God is real, and His Son Jesus is real, and I have experienced His salvation. His Holy Spirit is real, and I have experienced His infilling of His Holy Spirit.

December 10

The Wait

Psalm 27:14

Waiting on God requires time but also patience and trust. I have had occasion to wait for someone, sometimes for a long period, and I've worried that I might have misunderstood our time to meet or that the person was early and went on without me. Just like you, I have spent time waiting on God. The wait affords me the opportunity to better prepare for what God is going to do. If you are waiting on God for something in your life, then let me encourage you to spend the time preparing for what God is going to do. Believe me; it will be time well spent.

December 11

God's Plan

Hebrews 13:20–21

Two weeks prior to the birth of Jesus, Joseph and Mary made plans to travel to Bethlehem. Perhaps they had already started their journey. This was all in God's plan, but still, as humans, they had to *make* their plans and then carry them out. Perhaps Mary should not have traveled so far away from home that close to the end of her pregnancy, but go, she did.

In life, God has a plan for us, but as a part of that plan, He allows us to make our plans. Sometimes our work and life combine to force us to plan for travel, and we make those plans. God knows where we are at today and where He wants us to be in the future, and He arranges our lives to allow our plans to coincide with His. I have already made plans for extensive travel over these next two months. Most of these travel plans are work-related, with a missions trip back to Peru scheduled for mid-winter.

God knows where He wants me on specific days. I have made my plans, and I'm eager to see what God has in store. I think Joseph and Mary were eager to see God's plan unfold in their lives with the plans they had made. Life is a journey. Enjoy the trip.

December 12

Remind Me Later

2 Corinthians 6:2

"Remind me later" is a fact of our culture. Even our technology is equipped with this feature. We often put off things that need to be done and tell someone, "Remind me later." God's Word gives us an illustration of Jesus standing at the door, knocking to enter our lives. Many respond by saying, "Remind me later."

Time is short, and soon the time will be too far gone to remind you later. Open your heart-door today, while there is still time.

December 13

Changing Things Up

John 21:1-14

Our devotional last night covered the story of the fishermen who had toiled all night but hadn't caught a single fish. Jesus comes along and tells them to cast their nets on the other side, and they make the biggest catch of their lives. We read that Jesus calls them to follow Him and become fishers of men, and they cast their nets aside and follow Jesus.

Sometimes God will do a great thing in our lives and then ask us to go in a different direction. These men knew only fishing, and after the best night of fishing ever, Jesus called them into a different occupation. God may do something incredible in your life and then immediately ask you to move into something new. Will you respond like the disciples? Will you do what Jesus calls you to do? I trust that my faith is such that I will. How about you?

December 14

Out of the Mire

Psalm 40:1–3

Muck and mire are never fun to get into, yet at times, we find ourselves there. Others who have a broader view may see a way around the mire, but the view of a better path is blocked from our sight.

Yesterday I watched as someone attempted to cross a very soft area of shore and sank in up to his knees. I could see that if he had walked just a few yards farther, past some trees that were blocking his view, he would have had dry ground to walk on. From my vantage point it was clear, though this person couldn't see it. I called out to him to back out of the muck and go around, and I am glad he did.

Sometimes we make life choices that get us into mucky situations. God can see the whole picture and has identified a more stable path. Listen to His instructions as He calls out to you to go back and choose a different and better path.

December 15

Opportunity—Make the Most of It

Ephesians 5:16

Once again, our news is filled with the tragedy of violence poured out on unsuspecting people. Ephesians 5:16 shares this advice: "Make the most of every opportunity in these evil days" (NLT). Looking back to last week, what opportunities did I not make the most of? Looking ahead to this week, I desire to do better.

Lord God Almighty, as you direct my path, let me see the opportunities that come before me, as You see them. Help me to make the most out of them because we know that these days are evil. I have a spiritual sense that time is not just short but extremely short for the church of Jesus Christ to do good.

Join me in looking for ways to make the most of every opportunity to fulfill the great commission.

December 16

Instantly Ready All the Time

2 Timothy 9:2

God's Word advises us, as Christians, to be instant "in season and out of season." Let me relate this to my ordinary workday. When someone asks me which alfalfa variety would be best for their farm, that's an in-season moment for me, as I am well versed by my experience to answer the questions and make a recommendation. But then the questions turn to field-pest problems and how to control them. I know some of the products that work and when to use them, but I am not as well versed on application rates, and find myself "out of season." When someone looks to me for my advice and insight, I desire to be accurate and factual, even if I am out of season. In these circumstances, I will share what little knowledge I have and the experiences of others who have faced similar issues. Then my strongest advice is to seek out someone who works with these issues and work with them in addressing their pests. It usually is the person through whom they buy their nutrient and pest-control products.

As I share my faith and walk with Jesus Christ, my Lord and Savior, I will find that, at times, I am going to be out of season. But because the question or circumstance has come before me at God's discretion, it is important that I also trust God for help in how to respond. If God lives in my heart, then the Holy Spirit, who is instantaneous, also can speak through me.

It is humbling to speak not what you know but what God desires to speak into those lives. It is easy to wonder if these are my own thoughts or if they have been given by inspiration of the Holy Spirit. If I have drawn myself close to Jesus, and my relationship with God is strong, I have a deeper trust in hearing what God desires to speak through me. And yes, sometimes it is instantaneous.

December 17

Temporary Citizenship

Philippians 1:29

You probably are anticipating spending eternity in Heaven. If you are not sure about your eternal destination, make sure that you give your life to Jesus today, and let Him cleanse you of sin and make heaven your eternal home. But until we pass from this life, we are citizens of this earth. I sometimes wonder how life will be different in heaven than here on earth. Certainly, no sin or evil. No need for the sun because Jesus is the light that is needed. Certainly lots of changes.

In his letter to the Philippians, Paul states that we must live here on earth as citizens of heaven (Philippians 1:27). With this insight, how must I live differently, knowing that this is just a temporary dwelling place, and my real citizenship is in heaven? Paul's statement makes it plain: we "must" live like citizens of heaven. If I know that my actions and involvement will be significantly different when I get to heaven, then I need to make changes to my life here on earth.

One of the pictures of heaven in my mind is the throngs of heaven, gathered around the throne of God, giving Him glory, honor, and praise. I think that is one way we can live as citizens of heaven here on earth—by giving God praise, glory, and honor here on earth. Practice doing so here on earth. Don't let timidity keep you from doing so. If we will do this on earth, God has promised to open the floodgates of heaven upon our lives. I don't need to wait until I get to heaven to live like a citizen of heaven. I'm living the dream today.

December 18

Breaking the Chains of Evil

Romans 8:1-39

The evil desire of one human taking the life or lives of others has been around since the second generation of man, when Cain rose up and slew his brother, Abel. There was no gun, no bomb, no airplane, no weapon of mass destruction, only a sin-filled mind and a lack of will to walk away. Sin creates a growth chamber and a fertile environment for the depravity that grips a mind and leads individuals to act out the evil that enters their hearts and minds. Evil breeds even more evil, and we are witnesses to God's Word that tells us that evil is multiplied in following generations, even to the seventh generation.

The only thing—I'll say it again: *the only* thing—that can break that cycle is God's salvation of a sin-sick soul of an evil and depraved life, setting the person free of the bondage and chains of evil. Only God can break the chains of evil. Individuals cannot dictate it or create laws that will enforce the elimination of evil; only God can.

God, our culture and our generation needs you more than any previous generation to come and break the chains of evil that have us bound.

December 19

Organizational Filing

1 Corinthians 14:40

My favorite filing system is "file by pile." Many times when I've traveled, I have asked LaDonna to get something from my office and to give me the information from it over the phone. After her gasps of disbelief over being sure she cannot find what I sent her for and statements like "You need to clean your office," I'll direct her to one of my piles and tell her about how far down in the pile it is. Usually, in a short time she has mastered my filing system and has given me what I have asked for. She's good. But I am taking her advice and am cleaning my office, at the risk of not knowing where anything will be now.

Sometimes in life we get comfortable with our "piles," and when God says something about cleaning up, we have an automatic reaction that simply says, *I'm comfortable with my way of life and the disorganization that is a part of it.* I know from experience that I can become comfortable in my own mess. But God desires to take us to a new place, and sometimes organization or reorganization is needed.

Lord God Almighty, I want to follow Your commands all the days of my life. Help me to be obedient when You ask me to clean up my life. Really, I do want to be more like You, God Almighty.

Now, has anyone seen that folder I'm looking for—the one that used to be in the pile that was right here behind my chair?

December 20

Be the Church Using the Gifts of the Spirit

1 Corinthians 12:1–11

As I gather with others to worship in His house today, I have an expectation that goes beyond the normal expectation that God will be there and will meet us there. I am expecting that the power of the Holy Spirit will be present and that the gifts of the Spirit will be evident and powerful as we meet. What is God's desire for my church? To be His church and to open and use every gift of the Holy Spirit today. Yes, every gift, and yes, today. In His church—today.

December 21

If Time Is a Burden

Matthew 11:28–30

How have nearly fifty-one weeks of the calendar year flown by so quickly? Oh, I know that time flies when you are having fun, so I must have had a lot of fun. For some, though, time seems to be dragging, and the load they carry is overbearing. I know from experience that God is willing to take the burden off our shoulders and place them in His hands. All we must do is ask, then release those burdens into His care.

Satan's desire for you and your life is to see you mired down in sticky clay, nearly suffocated with your burdens. God's plan is to take your burdens, pull you out of the mire, and place you on a firm foundation, with joy, peace, and happiness in your life. Nothing will be perfect all of the time, but it's still immensely better than being in the pit. Give it to God.

Compelling Force

Luke 14:23

I very seldom share items I find on Facebook, but this morning one of my Facebook friends, Countryman Kabochi, posted this gem: "True Christianity is not a pleasure cruiser on its way to heaven but a battleship stationed at the very gates of hell."

God's Word instructs us to go into our world to "compel" others to come to Jesus for salvation. *Compel* is an action word that gives a sense of urgency and a need of immediate action. I consider myself as somewhat of a nice guy, and if I invite you to follow Jesus, but you tell me you are too busy, my natural reaction is to allow you the privilege of making that bad decision. I will go on and hope there will be another opportunity later because I don't want to offend or upset you. Yes, that's my natural reaction.

But today, I sense an urgency like never before, a compelling force to be a compelling individual to compel others to follow Jesus. Mr. Nice Guy is ready to be a compelling individual in the kingdom of God. I am working on my God-given directive to compel the lost to turn to Jesus. Time is short, and our lives for Jesus are stationed at the very gates of hell. We must compel those who are walking through those gates of hell to choose a different path—a path of salvation. Christian, work your station.

(Thank you, Countryman Kabochi)

December 23

Moved with Compassion

Jude 1:20–23

A quick look at those around us can be very revealing. I am not talking about the superficial look that most of us give but a look through the eyes of Jesus. While He walked this earth, Jesus could spot a leper from a great distance, a woman in desperate need at a well miles away, a demonic in the tombs from across the sea, and a multitude of hungry people in a wilderness area. I can easily and with just cause say, "I'm too busy to take time to see the needs of others." But Jesus took time. Oh, He was busy all right. You take twelve men and teach and train them. You might then understand why Jesus, very early in the day, would find a place of solitude and spend time with the heavenly Father.

Yes, Jesus was busy, but when He looked at humanity and the great needs that they were bound with, He had compassion upon them. But He went beyond just seeing the need. Jesus did something about it—every time. I don't have the resources to feed five thousand–plus hungry people, but I do perhaps have five bread buns and a couple of fish or some other bread and meat that I can give to Jesus.

I personally do not have a cure or remedy for disease, pain, or illness, but I know a healing Savior whose arm is not too short to reach down from heaven and heal everyone who needs the Healer's touch. I've noticed this about Jesus: He was not motivated by a desire to show off what He could do as the Son of God; rather, Jesus was moved by the compassion He had for those in need.

Lord God Almighty, let me see others in their need through Your eyes, and may I be moved with compassion to seek Your help, not to show what you can do but to alleviate the immediate need in the lives of those who so desperately need Your help today.

December 24

World-Changing Event

Luke 2:15–20

It was the eve of Jesus's birth. The world did not know it then, but it was about to experience a dramatic change in the next few hours. Consider this: from a historical point, the calendar would change from what we know as BC (before Christ) to AD (The Year of our Lord). God had not walked among humans since the garden of Eden. Now, God as man would live thirty-three years with humankind. In one life span, the multiple laws of the Old Testament would be replaced with two directives: (1) love God with all your heart, and (2) love others. No longer would people be required to offer a sacrifice for every sin committed. Jesus would become the final sacrifice, fully enough, for every sin, once and for all.

From a human standpoint, Mary had now carried Jesus in her body for nine months. A virgin, not having had any sexual relations, was told by an angel of God that she would conceive and would give birth to the long-awaited Messiah. It now was near the time for the birth, and with nine months of thoughts carried in her mind, she was on a journey to Bethlehem. Most likely, as a devout worshiper of God, she had reviewed as much as possible what the scriptures said about the Messiah. Where He would be born and how He would die are recorded in the Old Testament.

In the course of a few hours, the world would be turned upside down because God chose to become man and live among us. Perhaps today, your world is upside down, but you are the reason Jesus was born. Let Jesus turn your life right side up.

Proclaim Good News

1 John 1:1–10

Nearly all of us listen to or watch news during the day, not realizing that what we hear is tainted and often poisoned with the evil thoughts and desires of those who own, manage, and convey information to us. It seems that we don't hear news but propaganda, which is meant to divide our nation and destroy our godly principles. God's Word is truth, at times pure and simple and at other times poignant and complex, yet pure truth. If you are a pastor, prophet, evangelist, apostle, or teacher of God's Word, don't let the enemy of our souls water down, alter, or diminish the purity of truth found in God Word.

Even Christians are subject to having their ears "tickled" with part-truth, half-strength, adulterated information. We must preach and teach the full truth of God's Word, for it has power to save a lost soul. Preach it, brother and sister. Teach it, my friend. Proclaim it to the ends of the earth. God's Word of truth will set the captive free.

Today, we celebrate the birth of Jesus Christ, the Savior, the Messiah, the Redeemer, the Healer of every disease. Let's be like the shepherds and proclaim the good news to everyone.

December 26

The Day after Christmas

Jeremiah 29:11

It's the day after Christmas. The angels have gone back to heaven, the shepherds have returned to their flocks, and Joseph and Mary still must pay their taxes. Though the world was changed with the birth of Jesus, not too much of normal life changed. Flocks had to be tended, business had to be maintained, meals had to be prepared, and life returned to normal. In those first days, only God knew that Jesus's family would have to flee to Egypt to protect Jesus's life until the current ruler passed from the scene. Only God knew that He would place in Joseph's and Mary's hearts to make regular trips from Nazareth to Jerusalem to worship God. Only God knew what lay ahead thirty-three years later, as Jesus became our sacrifice.

But meantime, life went on. For us today, life goes on. Only God knows what tomorrow brings. The celebration of Christmas will soon evolve back to a normal life, whatever that may be. Yet because of Jesus's birth, life is not the same. Jesus—He's a life-changer. Let Him change your life today.

December 27

Good Advice

2 Timothy 2:1–7

As I near the end of this year and reflect on the Bible reading plan that I selected for 2016, I see that I am on track for the year, meaning that I have read everything for each day for the last 357 days. This year, my reading plan was the Chronological Bible. Today's reading was 2 Timothy 1–4. The apostle Paul is giving wisdom advice to a young preacher named Timothy. Paul shares that it is important, even vital, to read God's Word and to know it. In so doing, it will give direction in life.

For anyone who is wandering today, Paul's advice still stands. God's Word will provide guidance and direction. I can tell you that the occasional opening of God's Word does not replace a daily routine of reading God's Word. A daily, systematic, all-inclusive feeding of God's Word is just what we all need. Give yourself a wonderful Christmas gift that you can use every day of the year. Buy or subscribe to a Bible reading plan. There are many free ones online. Type in "Bible Reading Plans" in your search engine. I use Bible Gateway. It's free, and I enjoy the many options that it provides. Do it! You will be glad you did.

December 28

Filling the Void

Psalm 63:1–8

Boy howdy, that left a big void. A void is an empty place that was once filled or should be filled. I had to have a tooth pulled earlier this week, and either that molar was quite large, or my tongue is very small, but there is a big void in my mouth now. My mouth was designed to have that void filled, but now it is empty (but I feel better).

There is a void in each of our lives. That void was made for Jesus, and when Jesus fills that void, there is completeness and perfection. If Jesus doesn't fill that void, and we try to put other things there, we find ourselves not only uncomfortable but incomplete.

The first thing they did when the tooth came out was to make sure nothing remained and then placed some gauze on top and told me to keep it there for the rest of the day. Oh yes, it filled the void, but it was annoying and uncomfortable, and it was a great moment to finally take it out that evening. The void is still there, and my tongue can't seem to stop examining that empty place. I think I will get used to it while it heals, but there is a huge void that needs to be filled. Thanks to modern medicine, I can have an implant and crown placed in that void later, and the void will be filled with something designed to fit the space exactly.

Jesus fits the God void of your life exactly. Let Jesus remove the stuff that doesn't belong, and let Him fill His rightful place in your life today. I guarantee that removing what doesn't belong there and filling that void with Jesus will be the best thing that has ever happened to you.

December 29

Doing What I Know I Should Do

Romans 7:13–20

The apostle writer shares with us this insight about himself that he didn't do the things he should do and did the things he shouldn't do, and as I look at my own life, I can identify with him. I find myself doing the things I know I shouldn't do and not doing the things I know that I should do. How often we find ourselves doing exactly that. I know that I should exercise more, but I find myself making excuses for not doing so. I know that taking that second piece of pie will impact the scales even more, but it is so delicious that I give in.

We may know the importance of daily Bible reading and spending time with God in prayer, but we do not discipline ourselves to do so, yet we take time to watch something that's borderline distasteful on TV or spend time on Facebook or Snapchatting in place of the time we should spend with God. Intimate relationships start with spending time with one another. We will never have an intimate relationship with God if we don't spend time with Him.

Let me encourage you to spend time with God every day. I suggest early in the morning, and if your day is already filled to capacity, then set the alarm to wake a bit earlier.

How much time? I would suggest that you select a Bible reading plan that gives you specific portions of God's Word for every day. These range from reading the entire Bible in a year, to reading the New Testament in a year, to a lot of other options. You can find several options at the Bible Gateway website. Reading plans can take a few minutes to several minutes. I would suggest asking God which plan to select and then committing yourself to do this every day at the same time. Make it a habit.

I then would suggest committing additional time in prayer after Bible reading. It doesn't have to be an extensive amount of time, but it should be enough time to offer personal praise and thanksgiving, offer up requests, and then enough time to hear from God. Remember that prayer is a two-way conversation. Give God time to speak as you spend time communicating. If you are not spending time in personal devotions with God today, I encourage you to make it a priority and a new habit. You know that you should do it. Just set aside your own desire, and make yourself do what you know you should do.

December 30

Filling Our Minds and Lives with the Right Things

Philippians 4:8

We fill our minds and thus our hearts and souls with so many things. Whatever we have developed passion for in our lives is a result of what we have filled our minds with. The apostle Paul writes these words:

> Whatsoever things are true, whatsoever things are honest, whatsoever things are just, whatsoever things are pure, whatsoever things are lovely, whatsoever things are of good report; if there be any virtue, and if there be any praise, think on these things. (Philippians 4:8)

These are the things with which we should fill our minds and thus our hearts and souls. I believe we can safely assume that any act of terror committed by any one individual or group of individuals was committed, in part, because the things listed above were not a part of their thoughts. When you consider that the thoughts of the enemy of our souls are to hurt, kill, and destroy, you can easily see how our culture has been infiltrated with evil passion for hatred and killing. The mind is a war zone, and if the enemy can plant seeds of doubt, fear, and hate, he will take advantage of doing so.

Filling our minds with good things and the things of God is a choice that we make. Push out those things that do not appear in apostle Paul's list above, and concentrate on the things that are listed. I believe life will be better if you do.

December 31

I Need Wisdom

James 1:2–5

The Word of God declares that when we ask God for wisdom, He gives us wisdom. It's critical to know when we lack wisdom. In my mature years, I find myself asking God for wisdom in many things. Looking back on my life, I wish I had asked more often in my youth and young adult life. Asking God for wisdom is not being weak or noncommittal. It is simply knowing that I do not know the future or the outcome, while the one I ask wisdom of does know, to the finest detail. My asking God for wisdom is a significant sign of *wisdom*.

Lord God Almighty, Your wisdom is far superior to mine, and I can fully trust in Your wisdom.

As I approach a new year, may I seek wisdom that comes from God. May I not be bashful in asking God for His wisdom, counsel, and advice.

Printed in the United States
By Bookmasters